RELIGION TO REALITY

TERRY THOMAS

 BOOK PUBLISHERS NETWORK

Book Publishers Network
P.O. Box 2256
Bothell • WA • 98041
PH • 425-483-3040
www.bookpublishersnetwork.com

10 9 8 7 6 5 4 3 2 1

Printed in the United States of America

LCCN 2011910381
ISBN10 1-935359-89-4
ISBN13 978-1-935359-89-0

Editor: Julie Scandora
Cover designer: Laura Zugzda
Typographer: Stephanie Martindale

CONTENTS

FOREWORD

first noticed Terry Thomas when he sent me an email politely correcting a Bible reference I'd made in church. I'd seen him before, of course, in the audience paying attention to what I might be sharing on any given Sunday and shaking his head in agreement, but with that particular email I really took notice of him as a fellow Bible student with a deep commitment to gaining a greater understanding of this thing we call God.

Since that time, I've had the opportunity to be with Terry at retreats and in classes and was always impressed by his humble wisdom and inquisitive nature. I've never had any doubt that his pursuit of the Divine is foremost in his heart and mind.

Reading his book allows me into the back story of a man whose love of God stayed central in his life while the form of worship and connection was in transition. Reading his story helps me understand why I've always felt a sacred kinship with him. I, too, have watched my "form" of worship shift dramatically as I sought an outward teaching of God that would match my inner experience. I think this book will resonate with many who are questioning their religious roots and traditions because the answers to their questions didn't fit the religious box they had previously adhered to.

You are in for a good read.

Rev. Kathianne Lewis, D.D.
Senior Minister & Spiritual Director
Center for Spiritual Living – Seattle

INTRODUCTION

"**T**erry, get going; you have too much to share to keep it to yourself."

Yes, I had done it before, and I knew I could do it again.

Decades before, I'd written *At Least We Were Marrried* about a horrifying tragedy and the steps I had learned to get myself up off the mat for another round of life. My message of hope had touched hundreds of thousands. After publication, when I was speaking to people about the book, one question popped up more than any other: "What happened next, Terry?" I couldn't write it then because I was living the story and couldn't sort out what was happening in parts of my life well enough to make sense of it. So, I put writing aside and continued on with life while exploring myriad religious and spiritual channels.

But in a typical synchronistic moment, as I sat at my computer in Redmond, Washington, I happened to look through the daily articles on the Biznik Web site—a local site supporting budding entrepreneurs. A brief article by a young woman from near Dallas, Melanie Davis, caught my eye. Gathering outstanding stories to publish in an anthology, she was looking for contributors with unique, perhaps even captivating, stories of how they had recovered from a devastating grief-causing experience. I put together four quick sentences of how my wife had been killed and what I had done to overcome the sorrow that had changed my life, and shot off the email.

Melanie emailed back immediately and wanted to talk to me. It didn't take long over the phone the next Tuesday for us to hit it off. Soon after, I wrote my chapter for her book, which she published eighteen months later.

Writing that one chapter for Melanie and her telling me to "get going" helped me realize I was ready to reexamine my life, my struggles with grief, and my spiritual experiences in the context of all I had learned about religion as a passageway to a higher spirituality. Melanie's call was like water priming a pump. I was ready to let the words flow and had just needed a nudge.

As I prepared to write this book, a friend told me, "Terry, you've come so far, but do not forget the people you came from." He meant for me to keep in mind those who are where I was at one time in my religious endeavors, practices, and beliefs. To help them advance spiritually, I needed to remember the process I had gone through from the beginning, what had held me back, how I had wanted change but yet struggled against it sometimes, as well as what had helped me along.

I resonate to how the powerful theologian of the last century, Pierre Teilhard de Chardin, introduced himself in one of his books. "I in no way believe that I am better or more important than any other man: It simply happens that for a number of accidental reasons my own case is significant, and on that ground it is worth recording."

Like Teilhard de Chardin, others tell me they benefit from learning about my experiences, my explorations, and especially, my revelations. I believe my life's purpose, stirred up by that horrible auto accident, was to go out and explore religion and spirituality. But I found the two are not the same thing, not at all. At its best, religion keeps moving us along to a reality higher than itself—like a signpost on the interstate, pointing to new destinations—to ultimate spirituality. But, too often, religion falls far short and thinks it is the destination. I had had such hopes in religion. But even with advanced religious studies—a first-class PhD in theology—and an intimate understanding of religion—especially from the Christian perspective,

I found that it tends to keep us in a box. With few windows for fresh air and greater possibilities and with few doorways showing us the way past itself into new realities, we remain confined to a fixed set of beliefs—until we, ourselves, take action. To move into that higher spirituality when religion fails us, we must break out into our own thinking, I found out. And so I did, and my grief forced an opening in that box. I peeked out, looked around me, and discovered a way to spiritual consciousness. I still enjoy many things from religion, and I will show that in the story, but I've had to use it for what it is worth and move forward spiritually. And it turns out that what I found can now serve as a guide for multitudes who want to find a higher and more meaningful life on their own personal paths.

The ideals from many religions flow through me, now more openly and broadly, especially unconditional love and forgiveness. The more I manifest love, the more love I receive. Giving unconditional forgiveness to everyone—family and friends as well as those who oppose me—gives me power to live true to myself, in freedom, and with a purpose. Above all, loving and forgiving give me a sense of peace and acceptance. And I want this for everyone in his or her own way. I am on the path, my personal path, but the destination is still far ahead. In fact, knowing as many great people as I do, I don't believe anyone has "arrived," and the sooner we recognize that, the more able we are to get into our own destiny and onto our own path and stay on it. I have found the path for me, and it feels good.

My primary goal with this story is that readers find insight for themselves. You may be asking questions similar to mine or, maybe, you are just beginning to wonder if life offers more than what you are finding right now. Whether you have a religion or not doesn't matter for my story. What matters is do you feel that the path you are on will lead you to ultimate life fulfillment. Or is something still missing? Are you honest and comfortable enough to take a good look for self-examination? Are you living in total freedom to be who you are truly meant to be? Do you feel you are doing what you came to earth to do?

Those questions I have asked myself in writing this book, and the process has humbled me. I have gone back through time to see that I progressed from complicated religion to a simple spirituality. And, along the way, I found joy—a deep happiness from inside me. It feels very good. I have a daughter who said to me recently, "Dad, you are the happiest I have ever seen you, and that makes me happy, too."

The bottom line is this book not a book about how to be like someone else—me or Mother Theresa or even Jesus. This book is about finding what is holding you back from living in your personal destiny, overcoming the inevitable barriers, and becoming the true you—that genuine, eternal, authentic inner you. It is about the deeper good in you, rising to the surface, the you within that you may hardly know, what you've possibly kept covered your whole life. I believe you are good, you are perfect in your spirit, and you are better than you think you are.

As I open my own life to you, I echo the wise words of Elizabeth Lesser, a beautiful human being and author of *Broken Open: How Difficult Times Can Help Us*, "Opening up the secret of our human nature, revealing to ourselves and to each other our deep and soulful longings, our fear and sadness, our joy and wonder, is the critical step on the spiritual path. It is the step that makes the difference between living our own, real spirituality or just acquiring someone else's beliefs."

I reveal to you my story and life that you may more easily discover your own unique path of spiritual enlightenment and its glorious benefits.

CHAPTER 1

When suffering comes . . . that is when people begin
to seek a way out and to reflect about the meaning of
life and its bewildering and painful experiences.
                                        Carl Gustav Jung
                                        Psychiatrist

Despite the circumstances, this story reveals joy at its deepest, at the subterranean level of the soul. I have to look at it that way for it can also feel grim, and certainly, I have felt sadness. But all who hear it react differently. The story filters through everyone's personal experience, and although individuals' reactions vary, everyone has a gut-wrenching response. I've seen people cry; I've also seen people look toward the heavens and express gratitude. Sometimes the same person has both reactions and even at the same time. Most people say they come away better for having heard it. I know I have in living it, and I have felt the full rainbow spectrum of reactions and with intensity. As I reflect on this story, hearing myself tell it, coming up with more questions than I can, perhaps, yet answer, I also realize the story continues. This part but reflects the first steppingstones along my journey.

Come, walk with me a bit.

꒷

Rolling southward along Interstate 75 towards Florida at about six fifteen on that Saturday evening after Thanksgiving, twenty-three-and-a-half hours after Nancy's and my wedding, I smiled contentedly to myself. Life had blessed me with so much—a joyous celebration the day before, the most wonderful woman in the world now beside me, a future filled with hopes and dreams. As if to agree, nature displayed a glorious yellow-orange sunset, spreading wide in the west.

Beside me, Nancy had almost drifted off into a light slumber, but I couldn't let her go completely before saying for the third time that day, "I can hardly believe we are really on our way—finally!" Keeping my eyes on the road, I used my thumb to twist the new wedding ring on my left hand once again. How incredible it felt finally to be married.

When she didn't respond, I glanced over to the passenger seat and saw the bouquet of red roses tucked between her legs and what seemed to be a slight smile on her face. A smile like no other, it sent shivers of joy through my body, even then with her eyelids fallen over her beautiful blue eyes.

The day before, while everyone else had been putting the finishing touches on the plans for the ceremony, my best man, Irwin, and I had smuggled a dozen long-stemmed roses into the hotel's honeymoon suite for Nancy later that night. I loved springing her with little unexpected treasures. And she loved the surprises, which made them all the better. I can still hear her voice that night, with her slight Southern accent, as she walked through the door and discovered the roses. "Oh, Terry!"

When it came time to leave the next morning, she insisted on bringing the flowers with us. The only place they'd fit in our small car was on the floor, where the blossoms spread out between her knees, as though lying in her lap. I knew she did this as much for me, letting me know how she appreciated my gift, as for herself, keeping close the reminder of my love for her.

And I couldn't help but think about this wonderful woman who had agreed to share her life with me. Nancy's heart and soul possessed an incredible depth and a deep connection with God that revealed itself in her genuine love for everyone. In conversations, she listened with intensity and made each person feel he or she was the most important one in the world. But she never took herself too seriously. Nancy adapted to any person or situation, and she balanced her strong beliefs with a light surface of good humor and joy. Her cute contagious laugh came out easily and naturally because she so loved all of life. She fully appreciated her parents, so grateful for all they had done for her, and treated me like a king, as her mother treated her dad. Always ready to hold my hand. Always eager to see me.

Did I speak of her physical beauty? Every time I saw her pretty face that always had a smile or grin for me and her attractive five-foot-three figure that blended well with mine at six foot, my mind jumped its tracks.

The purity of her personality drew me, too, probably more than her physical attributes, because I believe physical and internal beauty of character flow together. I always felt something far deeper within her, a faith and wisdom under the surface I had never known in another, especially not in such a young person.

In case you haven't noticed, I was in love, and in love for great reasons.

And I was head-over-heels, sublimely in love that Saturday evening, as the dead-looking, brown and gray landscape of southern Georgia continued to slip past the car windows in those minutes as the sun set. I turned off the radio to meditate quietly on the wonder of the moment. Light rain fell as a sliver of sun still hung on the distant western horizon under the dripping clouds, letting descend an eerie veil over my otherwise joyous thoughts. Just enough moisture hung in the air that I had to turn on the wipers.

The atmosphere lent itself to musings, and my mind traveled back, to before the wedding, after we had become engaged. Nancy had told me how, when she was in high school, she had popped into her parents' bedroom one morning for something and noticed how they slept under the covers, all curled up and blended together. It looked as if there was only one person snuggled under the covers, she had said, and I think she was looking ahead to the time she would share a similar experience with me. As she had told me about her observation, I knew she could hardly wait for our wedding night.

I thought even farther back to almost two years earlier, to how my heart had leapt when I had seen her blue eyes for the first time. Her face had captured me, framed by her flowing brown hair tossed into a little flip at the end. The experience—*she*—had overwhelmed me, and my thoughts and feelings had jumbled around in me so I hardly knew what had hit me. I only knew something had moved quickly throughout me and I needed to pay attention.

Soon after we met, we had our first date. It was at Daytona Beach, the night before Easter, and we stayed up all night, talking, walking the beach, laughing, telling our stories, watching the sunrise. In our innocence, we felt there had never been anything like this first date between two people.

My mind focused again on my driving. The road ahead was quiet. I looked at the speedometer to see we were cruising at sixty miles per hour in a zone marked seventy. I shrugged. There was no rush. The past few days had been more than busy. Time now to wind down, I thought. On the island of Nassau, our honeymoon hotel room waited for us on the top floor with a stucco balcony overlooking the tops of the palm trees and white sands on the beach below. A wonderful place to play and get to know each other as husband and wife.

For the last time, I glanced over to the other seat and saw the finest and most wonderful person I had ever known. I still feel the moment, and I see it clearly in my mind's eye, even though years have passed. Relaxed in the seat and slumped a little towards me, her eyes closed and a bit of a smile playing on her lips, Nancy's beauty and the peaceful look on her face struck me and has stayed in my mind and thoughts forever.

I glanced in the rearview mirror to see no other car, no head-lights, nothing behind us. Nothing ahead either. We had the road to ourselves. Still, I felt the need to fiddle, and even though the eerie early evening light meant I didn't need to turn on the headlights just yet, I reached over and flicked them on anyway.

Out of nowhere, a set of glaring headlights, the likes of which I had never seen before or could ever have imagined, sped erratically into view, racing directly towards us in the opposite lane, having just come down an onramp onto the northbound lanes of the interstate. I saw them begin to weave and waver, like streaks of starlight on a photograph taken by a wide-open lens aimed at the night sky.

I couldn't believe my eyes; the maniacal headlights were going so fast that there was no time to think, let alone act. I began to call Nancy's name to awaken her.

"Nan—"

I got no further. I can still hear my own voice calling out to her. "N … a … n—" I had never called her Nan, only Nancy, but this was the last thing her conscious mind heard, if she heard it at all. She never woke up.

I cannot relate this part of the story without feeling the moment once again—the stunning questioning as I saw the strange car lights aiming at us and the piercing grief in losing Nancy without so much as a goodbye.

In the flash of a split second, those weaving lights barreled out of control at ninety miles an hour, flashed down into the median strip between us, jumped up the small incline onto our lanes heading south, and struck us head-on. No instant even to slam on the brakes.

As the lights leapt from the median and confronted us, the only thought I had was of confusion. What was happening?

The vision of those wavering lights would come back and haunt me night after night after night for months, even years. Sometimes I woke up in a sweat. It took years for those nightmares to leave me completely.

But what actually happened that night on that slick highway just after sunset?

In short, Nancy died instantly, but they pulled me from the car first. On this side of death, at least, she never knew what hit her.

But what about the other driver, the nineteen-year-old who thought he'd see how fast his car could go on that Saturday night? How was he doing? He had only a small injury to his ankle. Hard to figure, I think. His insurance was meager.

The experts could not explain why I lived yet Nancy died. In fact, they said I had gotten the worst of it because, at the same time that I lurched forward into the black steering wheel, the crash caused the steering wheel post to be driven directly out about six inches from its shaft, like a framing carpenter nail, and into the center core of my sternum. We went from sixty miles per hour to a dead stop. Nancy, on the other hand, had no steering post driven into her, yet she died. Why? Why she and not I?

And why did the accident happen with such exact precision? No other cars were in sight in either direction. Why ram into us head-on? Why not a hundredth of a second earlier or later and miss us entirely? Or maybe even a thousandth of a second? When had I ever heard of a car crossing the median like that and being so out of control? Never. Why us? Why at that exact moment? Why, WHY, *WHY*?

I had no answers at the time, and the questions gnawed at me until I found an acceptable way to answer them.

At the moment of impact, I was struck with immeasurable pain throughout my body. I felt it in my face. Both arms turned numb. I recall a horrifying feeling of deadness throughout my chest. My legs felt all smashed up.

When the car struck us, no one else had been on the road. And no one else appeared for some time. Eventually, one car did stop, and someone got out and looked in on the driver's side. I must have rolled my eyes or moved slightly in some way because he started yelling, "One's alive; one's alive!"

Still, we remained, and so did the pain. Before long, though, I wilted into total numbness—the blessing of shock settling in. Shock and pain drove me so deeply inside my mind that I had no wits to think or to feel anything.

More vehicles gathered. The wreck clogged up all traffic. Then, finally, help arrived. I heard the emergency personnel calmly decide my fate. "We'll take the other one first," they said, gathered around Nancy's side of the car after having pried off her door. Someone had to go to town to get bolt cutters to snip my seatbelt loose, and I remember the red lights flashing amid the stream of cars parked all over the road, shining their headlights on the crash scene. I didn't remember it for months, but later it came to me, years later, in fact, as the residue of shock washed away, that I saw and heard every movement as the police carefully and professionally worked in harmony to remove me from the car.

But the memory of one incident—a word that hardly does justice to the experience—has stayed with me forever and from the start.

They carried me into the ambulance, and throughout the ride, I drifted in and out of consciousness, never sure of reality as the nightmare of the accident replayed nonstop in my mind. As the ambulance neared the hospital, I gradually became conscious in the darkness of the back of the vehicle. Fully awake when we arrived, I was wheeled into the hospital's hallway. Beyond pain, I waited … and waited … and waited, lying on the gurney, for surgery.

In the midst of people rushing about, aware of my wrecked body, knowing a most horrible accident had ruined my dreams of a wonderful marriage, a most strange and wondrous miracle happened—a feeling of joy began in my body and spread out all over me, lasting at least one long hour. More than "touched" by God, I felt blanketed in his all-loving embrace and secure in the knowledge both that my destiny was fixed and that it was right and good. I had received a taste of a spiritual glory I would seek over and over, hungering for the whole banquet. This life-altering impact sent me on the spiritual quest I knew I had to follow. I now had a purpose, higher than any I had ever imagined before, that would pervade all that I would think and say and do from than moment on.

After that night, I would have to ask with all my questioning ability and seek through many false doorways and knock until I thought my life was a waste and the skin on my spiritual hands would be worn off before I found what ultimately healed me. It was a rugged journey, but I learned I had much to share. I found joy along the way, too, as I fit the pieces and meaning of my life into a new arrangement, one that would still unite Nancy and me and make me whole once more.

Nancy's purpose wasn't over—not at all. It would be up to me to carry her purpose forward, along with mine. Of the two of us, she was the most ready to die and to give her life, I believe, because if one of us was close to perfection, it was Nancy, not I. Although I didn't know it yet, working through various systems and beliefs to arrive at a new spiritual life would be my journey and my destination, and

I would do this not just for myself but for the benefit of others in the world who sought help in finding their purpose for their own lives.

Nancy would be there as a memory and an inspiration and, more important, as a spiritual guide to help me.

Meanwhile, the highway patrol located our parents, who were together at the Atlanta airport; my parents were moments away from boarding. A request for Nancy's father blared over the loudspeaker. "Mr. Groover, please come to a courtesy phone immediately."

Nancy's kind father always had a positive attitude, which served him well as a manager in life insurance sales. When he heard the announcement, he smiled at everyone standing in the waiting area, asked them to wait until he got back, and left to find the phone. He was gone a long time. When he returned, my parents said he was shaken, ashen, and could barely speak, but he told them, "There's been a bad accident. Terry's alive, but we don't know about Nancy." He did know; he chose not to say anything at the time. The four of them made a silent ride back to the Groovers' home, and the plane took off with two empty seats my parents would have occupied.

The hospital's Dr. Kirkpatrick called the Groovers' house soon after they pulled up, and he spoke on the phone with my parents. "We are taking Terry into operating. If you want to see your son alive again, get here as fast as you can." He hung up. And they did get there although it took hours because it was quite a distance away.

Three nights before the wedding, my father had had a premonition, which wasn't unusual since he'd had them throughout his life. This time, however, he didn't tell me until much later he'd had a terrible dream. Even then, he was so terrified that he never told me or anyone the details and carried them to his grave.

I think the premonition may have come to help prepare him for the moment when he and Nancy's father would pull into the wrecking yard and see our destroyed vehicle and all four parents would deal with Nancy's death and my physical trials.

I did recover eventually, obviously. Where my life led next was as much a surprise to me as it might have been to anyone. Some people tell me it is a wonder I am still sane. I wouldn't go that far, but I can say that in my search for answers, I have had a tough but rewarding journey. I have overcome the grief from a day with elusive and painful memories, but I have also touched again that ultimate joy as my heart has found its purpose and meaning in life

My physical recovery moved relatively quickly, given the extent of my injuries. In a matter of a year, I felt back to normal and was running three miles a day. But I did it one step at a time.

My spiritual and emotional recovery, however, was another story. It took years, despite starting with that hour or more of intense joy in the light on the gurney in the hospital hallway as the medical staff decided how to handle me. I didn't seek it. It came to me. I saw that I would live. I knew that I knew that I knew. No doubt, whatsoever.

Also, I was given the message that I had a definite purpose for living, and discovering what it was became a driving force in my life. My life had a purpose.

At that moment, it was as if I saw God.

Later, I felt incredibly frustrated, knowing I had a purpose but not being clear on what that purpose was. I tried various things and discovered, at times, I had been misled. I would think I was on the right path and, instead, find out it was only temporary. Sometimes, and in some places, I lacked confidence and wondered where to go next. At other times, I was overconfident and fell flat. I also had horrifying disappointments, bad enough to turn me around from the misdirected path I was heading down. Then I would have powerful moments or promising experiences, which lifted me just enough to keep me going.

I did know that, when I found my purpose, it would have the same magnitude of spiritual consciousness as I had had on that gurney. But I wasn't looking for a momentary flash of light from heaven. I embarked on a search for a consistently uplifting life. One by one, the pieces came together, and as they built upon one another, the greatest enlightenment came almost all at once within a twenty-four-month span, and this, years later.

When I eventually felt I might have one reason why I had lived and Nancy had died and what I should do with my life because of it, I discovered that this ultimate spiritual high was more of an expanding plateau than a mountaintop, and that it was something I could live on for the rest of my life. Although this level fell short of the ultimate high, it sat so much above where I had spent my life until then—and where most of us spend all of our lives—that it gave me incredible joy in each moment of every day. I also discovered I could help others reach the same place. And maybe, just maybe, we could even venture beyond to that ultimate high.

Back then, however, in the early days after the accident, I felt as if I was a newborn cell splashed upon an unknown, exposed beach, struggling and evolving into something greater with an immense desire to survive and find my highest potential. Thrown into an entirely new life, I now had to learn how to live. Yet I had also briefly experienced an incredible spiritual awareness that I craved and wanted on a permanent basis.

What about Nancy? She had wanted a groom, a wedding, and to be married. She had had all that, some of her friends reminded me, and some have said that she died in her finest hour. Maybe she had, but I missed her terribly; I felt cheated. Ultimately, over the next year and a half, I would have to try to say a firm goodbye in my heart to Nancy.

CHAPTER 2

A real friend is someone who walks in when the rest of the world walks out.

Proverb

I'll lean on you and you lean on me and we'll be okay.

Dave Matthews Band

After the grand spiritual high on the gurney in the hospital hallway, the last thing I expected was nightmares. But the morning after, the same one I'd had in the ambulance on my way to the hospital the night before kept replaying in my head—the glaring headlights of the car were streaking at us, when the doctor woke me to tell me that my wife was killed in the accident. Again and again, it coursed through my mind like an endless tape. Over and over. Night after night. And during the day when I'd fall asleep. Two headlights racing at me, two blinding light streaks rushing through the dark, and just when they'd crash through me, they would back up and start over. If only I could locate a switch, I'd shut the wretched nightmare off.

I wanted to relive that good experience on the spiritual high—not the horrific car crash. But in those early days, I had no idea of the grief I would soon face and what it would take to walk through it. I also had no tools to understand the tension created between the distress at the bottom of the valley and the spiritual mountaintop. That stress, however, played a big part in what launched me in my spiritual search and brought me to where I am today.

Before I could find that proverbial pot of gold at the end of the rainbow, I had to live through the nightmares. But they created a surreal void of gray around me, which made grasping reality that much more difficult. How could I believe Nancy was dead? I'd vacillate between thinking it's true and, then no, it can't be. I lived in a wild world of imagination, unsure of reality. I even had dream episodes where Nancy was still alive.

Back then, though, I was like the lost soul in a cave, despairing of ever escaping the darkness of overwhelming grief and sorrow, wondering how I would ever discover the warmth and healing of sunlight. I knew only where I was—physically still in pain, far from recovered from my surgery, without my life-partner; emotionally, looking into the dark depths of sadness as I grappled with adjusting to my new reality; and spiritually, even with the gurney experience, wondering where God had gone to. I had no perception of where to go or how to get there. But step by step, I went from there to here. Some of the journey was good; some parts were not so good, but looking back, it all makes sense to me now. The path winds and meanders, sometimes sinking down into the valleys of life, other times rising back up to mountaintops, only to tumble down again. Twisting, turning, and making mistakes filled my journey. That's how I learned, over and over. I could sit despondently and dwell on what happened and feel Nancy's loss and the hurt of so many people forever, but to what end? What good would I be if I did not find happiness in my life to share and spread around with others?

Who really wants to be stuck in an emotional cave at the bottom of a valley?

Not I, and so I found a way out.

And once out, I knew I needed to go on into the higher reaches. I had tasted more than freedom from the depths of despair. I had also felt that night the goodness of God lifting me, the whole of me, above normal life and this physical world and into the arms of supreme love. I knew I would never be satisfied again without finding that ultimate spiritual life.

As I lay in that hospital corridor, with my body a complete mess—broken sternum, broken arms, smashed legs, lacerated face—I felt myself rise to the highest mountaintop. Miraculously, I will not die this night, I realized. *I will live.* I didn't consider the grim, skeptical attitude of those around me or any medical prognosis or what others said or demonstrated with their actions. I never believed that I would die. I would live—I knew this absolutely. It was something spiritual, from an invisible world: a voice and a vision that caused me to feel that way. I *knew* I would live.

And, above that, I received the knowledge that my life had a purpose. "I am living, and I have a great purpose to live," I had heard myself thinking as I stared at the corridor wall, which I still see in my mind. The words stood out as if written on the wall in big, bold, capital letters. Wherever this message came from, it made sure I couldn't miss it.

I knew at the time, however, and for years after that, that this unknown purpose was too important to fit into the normal things I would do along the way—business ventures, jobs, earning a PhD, and even the roles I had within ministry groups. Every activity was second to my overall search for my ultimate meaning and purpose. I meandered through religious ideas and organizations, crossing off one after another, hoping to find it in one of them because I felt that the greatest purposes in life would come from the world of God, which I thought of then as the world of religion. I tried this, then tried that, and nothing fit. Every theological proposition, every organization, and every effort seemed too small. The God that was always handed to me was too small. Nothing fit.

In my genetic make-up, my spiritual DNA or spiritual gift or whatever we might call it, I loved religion, but I also had the ability to see beyond the superficial surface and more clearly into the heart of it. I had the innate belief that religion should be genuine and authentic. But I began to see religion more like a game of charades, where people dressed a certain way, learned a certain language, and spoke the empty phrases. And the religion was actually void of any genuine new vibrancy that carried fully into daily life. Gradually, I learned I was to help others see the game they were playing and how it held them back from their purpose in life. Once they would release themselves from its grip, they could step into genuine living from a spiritual base.

Unfortunately, I hadn't even reached that point yet, even though I had tried. I saw the problem with religions' lack of authenticity, but I didn't really know where to go from there, how to find a genuine spiritual connection to God and the world. I couldn't lead blindly; I'd have to strike out on my own and discover the answers for myself before sharing them.

To find this spiritual connection—and then to live it and share it—was my purpose, my reason for living.

I have always loved religion. But I did not love that religion too often served the egotistic needs of leaders at the expense of serving the people. In my experience, I ultimately concluded that religious enterprises easily became structured organizations that spent their energy protecting and expanding their own power. This, to me, ran completely against the values I thought religion should represent. I had always felt religion should encompass an entire philosophy of life, but too often, religion concerned itself only with enhancing its own power, including setting itself as a mediator between we, the people, and God.

Eventually, I saw that I had to give up ideals, ideas, and beliefs that religion had foisted on me and had been blocking me. I also realized I did not have to give up all of religion in discarding its unhelpful trappings; I could still embrace the positive aspects while I let go of what did not serve me. But I say "eventually" because I needed time to see how religion, a source that should have worked to advance my spiritual development, actually slowed me down. And it does for most of us. But why? Why was I slow to give up some of those things I'd held dear? And what were they? Those answers would come to me in bits as pieces, always just enough for me to absorb and at just the right moment for me to hear.

Meanwhile, I had to heal my body and heal my heart over the loss of Nancy, not just to achieve balance then but also to allow me to move forward. It turns out the grief process was integral to my new journey. The pain of grieving was like the approach of a thunderhead, threatening to pour its fury out on my soul if I remained stuck; it got me moving in earnest. Accepting the sadness of my loss, discovering the tools to manage it, and then learning how to use them all acted as an insistent, world-shaking catalyst.

We did not have classes, books, or grief coaches back then. We were not schooled in what a grief process might look like. The previous generation had held a stiff upper lip through the poverty of the Great Depression and sacrifices of World War II, through failure, foreclosures, deaths of loved ones, and more that planted deep, deep sorrow in their hearts. But they learned to put the bad memories aside. They kept true to the American heritage of hope and a positive spirit. But my generation had none of those experiences as our foundation; we had basked in a charmed life, free of cares.

So when times of trial would hit one of us, we had little cultural experience to go on, little to guide us. We knew nothing of the typical signs of grief, such as shock, denial, bargaining, blame, anger, and depression, let alone how to handle them. But I was experiencing them all, seemingly alone. Actually, we didn't know enough to call it grief, then. About the closest thing to the word "grief" some of us knew was from *Peanuts* in its expression, "Good grief, Charlie Brown." But my grief was simply an overwhelming feeling of sorrowful sadness setting in. People visited me, which was often comforting, but I had no one I could speak to in confidence.

I wouldn't have known what to say, anyway. They would have had to ask key questions so I could ferret out my feelings. I now know this would be called depression. It was not a clinical, deep depression but more a feeling of hopelessness. What would I do? Where would I go? Where could I begin a new life?

Not knowing how to seek help or if it even existed for what I was going through, I knew I would have to figure out my own path, or I'd be dead in the water.

I intentionally decided to face the grief head-on, whenever possible. And so it began.

I learned that the pain would be a continual presence, perhaps throughout my lifetime. Later, I had better control over the physical pain. But I also noticed grief everywhere, sometimes unrecognized by those grieving, and this made me sad. As human beings, either we are losing something, or we are afraid we might lose something. When we do, we grieve. It doesn't have to be a large loss, like losing your wife to death. Little, unresolved griefs can add up until one day a trigger goes off, and we implode and fall into a deep depression. Or we fire off in an explosion of anger and commit an outrageous act from this pool of built-up, violent emotion.

Learning from experience, I found that grief is not something we "fix," but instead, it is a daily process we manage. Once we get the tools in our hearts to work with, caring for our grief issues becomes a skill we can use throughout our lives. I also learned that we can get better and better with practice.

And life gave me plenty of opportunities to hone this skill.

A couple of months later, back in the Northwest, after multiple surgeries at the hospital in Georgia, I was recovering at my parents' home. I was walking up to one-fourth of a mile a day and starting to feel that I was getting better, both physically and emotionally. Then, without warning, I began to feel blue. I was truly astonished at the bleak turn my emotions took as life slapped me in the face with a stunning new grief-reality, new to me, but I believe others who have had severe shock and grief have experienced something similar. Specifically, I would feel normal for short periods of time and think, "Well, I'm glad I'm feeling better now." But suddenly, without warning, a wretched, opposite, painful sorrow, accompanied with a shot of intense physical, internal pain, would strike me down emotionally—out of nowhere, as if a missile had hit me.

The pain in my body raged from the bottom of my throat, downward through the core of my torso. I felt a horrible tightening, as if I was being squeezed by some force, and it hurt. If I had known about breathing exercises then, they might have been helpful. But the worst of it was that I had no control over when or how long the deep grief-pain would last. I might have nearly one whole day of feeling fine, but then the next day, the opposite. Or it might change hour to hour.

My life got jerky. One minute I was fine. Then, suddenly, I was rattled, stunned with pain.

But this, too, I knew I could overcome, just as I was gradually coming to terms with the nightmares of headlights dashing at us. I had begun to accept them. The nightmares riled me and disturbed me, but each one was something I had been through before. And the time between each one widened.

One of the greatest tools I learned, one that anyone can do at any time, seems so simplistic now. I discovered the power of giving gratitude—especially when I felt the most sorrowful. Even if we do not believe in a higher power or God, just to say aloud, which I did sometimes, "To anyone out there listening, I'm mad and angry and depressed about what I have lost, but I am giving you thanks in this moment for life, for what I do have left, for what I did have, even if it is gone now."

Not that I gave thanks *for* Nancy's death, but I found help managing my grief when I was able to remember what we had had and be thankful for it. I even had moments when I gave thanks for having known her and married her, rather than complained and wept. For a few minutes, I was able to forget the loss and be happy for what I had had. In other words, when I was able to dwell upon the good I had had, instead of the good I was deprived of, I always felt better.

I guess it is like dropping a goblet of barely sipped, rare vintage champagne and seeing the precious liquid splattered on the floor with shattered glass. Having had the pleasure of tasting the fine champagne before breaking the glass and losing the champagne, my choice now would be to give thanks for the tastes I had had rather than turn bitter for not getting to finish the whole glass.

The normal pattern would be to complain, to cry out for what I didn't get, and I am certainly not immune to complaining, especially inadvertently. Complaining can be subtle and not easy to see in ourselves, so I learned to be alert and pay attention. Striving to live on the other side, the gratitude side, helped me manage the grief-terror that raged in my soul.

I was no angel. I was a student of overcoming grief, and I still am.

This doesn't mean I couldn't—and didn't—sit by myself and argue with God. In fact, once I was feeling better, I got almost overwhelmed with the question of *why*. If God was so good and all-powerful, how could he let something like this happen? I heard something one time that's stuck with me: "Either God is good and not powerful, or if God is powerful, he is not good." I couldn't argue with the sound and simple logic of that statement. And getting no good answer to my *why* did not help my sadness at the time.

So with the terror of the nightmares abating but the emotional upheaval of the pain-relief rollercoaster slapping me silly, I yearned for someone I could talk to, someone who understood and would listen and not make me feel stupid or helpless or like a failure. But there seemed to be no one.

Then, at the right moment, I was handed a magnificent and beautiful gift. It turned out there was one person I could talk with on a deep personal level who had experienced something similar and who understood.. And this person lifted my spirits, as I did hers.

Karen and her husband, John, were college friends of mine. They had married right out of college. John was a couple years older than Karen and I and was tragically killed in fierce hand-to-hand combat in Viet Nam just one week before Nancy was killed on the highway.

John and Karen were a handsome couple on campus. I remembered John's strong Swedish features, his blond hair that matched a strong, pronounced profile. He was one of those people you felt was a born leader. The news of his death shocked me. I couldn't believe it, couldn't wrap my mind around it.

Karen was also striking. Her long dark hair and olive complexion matched her deep brown eyes and reflected her heritage from the Mediterranean coast of southern France—a great contrast to John's Nordic features. Karen and I shared some classes and had become good friends several years earlier because we'd always had much in common. Her cheerfulness and soft smile made laughter easy whenever we joked around. She was also particularly smart.

Once I got back to the Northwest, Karen called after reading of Nancy's death in the papers. She hadn't even known I was engaged, let alone married. Because of our recent tragedies, we were supportive of one another and a great gift to each other. She drove up to see me several times because I couldn't go out of the house yet. So we visited in my parents' den and talked for hours. I had casts on both arms, still looking like an invalid, and Karen sat, all pretty and proper—what an odd pair we were! Yet we were both hurting tremendously. Our conversations went all across the board—from telling each other of our joys in the past to discussing our heartbreaks to pulling out anything else we wanted to talk, laugh, or even cry about.

What a heart-warming gift this was.

She described her sorrow, which started the moment she saw a highway patrol car in her driveway as she returned home from teaching school. She knew instantly what that meant and the news the policeman brought. Military wives *knew*.

Fortunately for me, Karen had a way of speaking about things with a smile. She didn't cry or beg for sympathy when she told me about that day and her sorrow.

"We have so much in common, Karen," I said one evening.

We did, and in another time or place, our intimacy might have led in a different direction. We were sharing so many deeply personal thoughts, we had known each other for some time, and both of us felt such a tremendous emptiness inside. And yet, neither of us had any desire to fill that gap any time soon. We still had healing to do, and I think we both felt no one could replace our lost loves.

"I know, Terry," she said thoughtfully. "Do you feel ups and downs like I do?"

"Karen—I do. How did you know? One day everything seems normal to me, like old times, and then other days hit me with real downers. It's all mixed up. I will forget everything for a while, and then I'll see Nancy's picture or think of some moment we shared. And down I go."

"It seems so strange, Karen, to think of you as a widow," I said, focusing on her.

"I know, but you are a widower, Terry; don't forget."

It sounded so stark. No one had said this to me up until then. Married for less than a full day but still classified as a *widower*. But she was right—I couldn't forget why I had that new, wholly undesired title. "How could I ever forget? Nancy was the most wonderful person I've ever known. You would have loved her. John, too."

Our conversations helped us both to realize we weren't going crazy and our topsy-turvy feelings might be normal after going through what we had each experienced.

One evening, Karen said, "Terry, I'm pretty sure that I'm taking a trip to Europe by myself next summer, just to get away."

"You are?" I asked. I looked up at the ceiling and thought for a moment. "What a wonderful idea." Getting away on an adventure, I thought, might help me overcome this horrible feeling of grief. "Hey, Karen, I don't know if I'll be in any condition to travel by summer, but if I am, I might make a trip, myself, now that you mention it."

"Good idea," she said with a fresh spark in her eyes. "I think that would be great. Let's keep in contact."

We continued to talk from time to time and discussed how to coordinate schedules. It was too early for me, though, to make anything definite.

Meanwhile, during the gray days that submerge the Northwest in winter, I began to ask questions I had not asked before, ones I hadn't been able to face prior to that point.

What was I to do now?

Where would I start?

Who was I before I had met Nancy?

What had changed about me?

Could I go back to life as it was?

I had a partial answer for that last one: probably not. But I had to consider it. I was facing an entirely new life that could never be the same as it was or as I had wanted it to be, but isn't that true for all of us from time to time?

As I asked these questions and tried to figure out who this new person was, this widower Terry, I realized I needed to return to my roots—to re-examine the person I had been in my youth and how I had grown to become the man I was before Nancy's death.

I was digging up old childhood pictures and remembered how unusual I was as a kid because I loved to spend hours sitting outside on a mound of dirt, entertaining myself. I was happy being outdoors, in nature, I realized, and recalled regularly losing myself in my own imagination as I hung out in the grass and dirt, watching the clouds changing in the sky and playing with sticks, garter snakes, worms, trees, and anything else out there to put my hands on. You would never have found a happier little boy; that's who I was.

I also discovered I had always felt like a misfit. My family members were all extroverts by nature, and I was more introverted. I needed space alone, even as a child. On camping vacations, I would wander out in the woods alone. I simply needed that time, but my family would say, "Where's Terry? What's wrong with Terry?" Nothing was wrong; we just didn't realize then that we are all born with different personality needs.

One time, I ran across a wise sentence by writer Elizabeth Lessing that encouraged me: "I recently heard a great writer say that an essential element in the life of a writer is to have been an outsider in childhood, to have been given the 'gift' of not belonging."

She had me to a T, a two-, three-, four-, or five-year-old, lying back in a clump of grass, all alone on those warm summer days, having a wonderful time, and looking up at the blue sky with a whiff of a white cloud floating here and there. I remember thinking, "I wonder who God is." "Who am I?" "Where did I come from?" "What is life for?" "How big is God?" "Are we just little ants under the footsteps of a giant?"

It's no wonder I was attracted to philosophy courses in college and made it my major. That's also a lonely study because it requires the student to do his own thinking. It is a little different from the hard sciences, where we do experiments and record the results rather mechanically, sometimes.

Having read that liberating sentence that described not belonging as a gift, I thanked Elizabeth for the permission to be me and for the acknowledgment of how it fit into my path. I knew I was closer to my destiny now and felt okay to sit alone at my desk and think, my outer, more defensive self now ready to share with my inner, more intimate self.

This gift—my history of introspection and ability to go contentedly my own way—undoubtedly aided my recovery in many ways, and it has led to the discoveries I've made about healing and grief and spiritual awareness.

But more from my childhood needed to be examined and assessed—more limiting beliefs that held me back and prevented me from reaching that spiritual high I so desperately sought and needed in the months after the accident.

CHAPTER 3

Guilt is never productive. It will stand in the way
of achieving your goals. So get rid of this emotional
barrier to success.

Jack Canfield
Author, *Chicken Soup for the Soul*

n those dreary days recovering at my parents' home in the Northwest, I took stock of my life. I had no home of my own now, as I'd had at college and had planned with Nancy. Uncertainty lurked ahead. I had been pursuing a spiritual life, including evangelical work while at college, and had intended to continue in that direction with Nancy. And I'd had a taste of a career in ministry on campus while Nancy was still a student at Georgia Southern and I, a staff person at Kansas University. But I no longer had enthusiasm for it, couldn't focus on it; the zest had just slipped away for me.

Where would I go? What would I do?

Lying on the gurney in the hospital a few hours after the car crash, I'd had something like a vision, intensely clear yet also without details. I knew my purpose was big, and I knew it was important. This was more than feeling. It was something that got into my deeper soul and drove me into my life's search in the spiritual arena of life. Even without a clear purpose, the sense I had one drove me to recover ahead of the doctor's prediction and anxiously jump back into living. Frustrated and puzzled, I wanted to know where I was headed. My life needed restarting.

But who was I? What did I like? Where was I from? What influenced me the most? These were questions I realized I needed to ask and answer as I started forward in a new life.

I had the time. I had the resources. I had the motivation. I wanted self-improvement, which to me meant to bring spiritual awareness more fully into my life. So I delved into a review of my early and formative life to understand better who I truly was as a person.

My discovery stunned me. I came face to face with a fierce enemy, one rarely acknowledged let alone confronted and surmounted—a deep and tightly gripping sense of guilt. I saw how it had been planted in me, only to grow out and circle around me like a choking vine. And I saw this same guilt thing in many other people, tightening around them just as powerfully and more completely than any of us had ever realized. If I wanted to keep moving forward as I had been doing for a few years by now, I knew I would have to overcome this guilt that stood in my way to spiritual advancement.

Because the problem is so common, it was hard to spot. So integral a part of our life—like the air surrounding us—we don't recognize it or pay attention to it. That made it all the harder to deal with. I found little help when I began, so I pretty much went by the seat of my pants, and it became a lifetime process. Few people, if any, know how powerfully, completely, and insidiously guilt infects us. I also learned that guilt twisted through religion in the Western world for fifteen hundred years. We inherited it, but I found we could break its hold. And I would start not by pontifications but by example.

Examining guilt, both within me and in our whole culture, let me advance in my journey, and more important, it provided me with the reason for that spiritual quest. No longer relinquishing power to guilt, I found the power in spiritual consciousness.

Interestingly enough, just as the church of the Middle Ages planted guilt deeply into the Western world's consciousness, today's church sowed it in me. The church thought it was doing good and right, and perhaps because that long-running, deeply infecting consciousness of guilt weakened its ability to understand fully what was happening.

Humans are not made to feel guilty or be guilt-driven, I came to believe later, but only once I overcame the latent guilt deep in my own psyche.

My discovery began with a return to my childhood. I looked at the influence of the church on my life. I loved the church, and as I loved my parents and took their word as gospel, so I absorbed the church's word as truth. As children, we naturally take in the world given to us—television commercials, cartoons, radio programs, what we hear at home, in school, from friends, or from the culture in general, as well as messages conveyed to us by any church we attend. We are deeply bathed in them, immersed. As Dr. Maxwell Maltz says, "It is no exaggeration to say that every human being is hypnotized to some extent, either by ideas he has uncritically accepted from others, or ideas he has repeated to himself or convinced himself are true." And who most of all is without critical thinking? Children. Children absorb what they are given.

Perhaps the words "imparted" or "provided" are gentler words for the process and less offensive than "brainwash," but I need to make the point clearly. None of us wants to think we were programmed to believe a certain way rather than accepted it because it made sense. But all cultures do this to some extent, passing such information on in a society through imitation or without conscious awareness. Some of it can benefit the people—how to nurse an infant, when to harvest crops, what plants heal certain ailments. But this method can also destroy or hurt the individuals—believing only men have the capacity for intellectual endeavors, mistrusting all people not of the group, seeing only harm in any innovation, even medical advances. From a religious standpoint, I was taught I was a helpless sinner in thought, word, and deed—an unclean creature. I wasn't just dirty, as from mud and grass stains and sand on the outside that water could wash off; my very nature from the inside was unclean. Worse yet, reminders of my impurity were implanted every week, Sunday after Sunday.

The church did this in its sermons, each admonishing us to follow certain rules, telling us to behave correctly, and especially, emphasizing what we "should" do. I remember how I cringed at that word.

Even as a very, very small child, I had an instinct that something was wrong. "Guilt happens when you think words such as *should, must, ought to,* or *have to,*" declared Jack Canfield of *Chicken Soup for the Soul* fame. "You will be more effective if you replace guilt-tripping with phrases such as *I want to ... It supports my goals to ... It would be smart to ...* and *It's in my best interest to ...*" The church made sure, perhaps without thinking, that guilt happened.

I had to learn that there was nothing I *should* do, nothing at all. Either do it or don't do it. As Bishop Augustine of Hippo said, "Love God and do what you will."

Adults can pick and choose what they hear and receive. But children? No, the ideas get implanted into our young thoughts, and guilt spreads through the mind. And what we think we are, we become. As prolific, spiritual writer Emmet Fox said, "If you believe that you are a miserable sinner and keep on saying so, that will be the best way to become one." What we say to ourselves about ourselves becomes truth to us, and we become what we say we are. And so the little children who accepted those thoughts grow into adults who have no idea that they have carried the guilt from childhood with them. The guilt has become so much a part of who they are that it rests safe and secure, unquestioned, undisturbed.

The church also implanted ideas of our unworthiness more subtly through its memes. Church memes can be the toughest to identify and destroy because they are associated with God, the highest, holiest judge and authority there is for a child. To embed the memes more firmly, doctrines often came in the context of emotion-stirring music. The combination of hearing the words, speaking them in song, and feeling them with the heart stamped those ideas deeply into the souls of the little ones.

To make the process even more challenging to undo, by the time the memes are living out life in the person as an adult, the programmed concepts seem absolutely normal and right. After all, doesn't everyone hold the same or similar beliefs? We can't all be wrong.

Or can we? Unless we work diligently to uncover these basic beliefs, we will have no idea of the impact they have on our lives, how guilt holds us back from a joyous life and impedes our spiritual growth. I found I would have to do the difficult work of bringing my doctrines planted in me into my consciousness if I was ever to attain higher spiritual awareness—in short, to have the best relationship with God possible for me. And that would mean removing all trace of guilt.

Sermons even children could tune out. So the church had other ways to plant the subtle messages into the mind and create lifetime, guilt-provoking habits. One came with the repetitious liturgy, a set of words that the people say together every Sunday. This ritual, like any, has the force of indoctrination, which means to get certain doctrines or teachings into a person easily and without thought. Like citizens singing their national anthem, we absorb the meanings behind the words more deeply with each repetition. And joining with others in singing "The Star Spangled Banner" embeds within us an emotional sense of history in the soul in a way that listening to a speech or reading a book cannot do. Saying the words of the liturgy, in addition to singing songs, provided the church with effective ways to instruct its members, and "indoctrination" was not thought of as pejorative. In my theological studies, a worship teacher advocated this method, saying that one reason for the liturgy was to teach the people. For children, if they hear it and repeat it often enough, it gets in them, and they stay in the church and keep believing the doctrines. Another teacher I was close to at one time said that, historically, the liturgy held the church together more than any other thing, and he thought this was a good thing and promoted it.

This ritual in my church service opened each Sunday with the liturgical words, "We confess that we are by nature sinful and unclean and have sinned you in thought word and deed." Then the pastor said we were forgiven, but the forgiven part didn't seem to make much impact.

Just as with the ABC song or a commercial jingle repeated over and over, once a child gets words and ideas in his or her brain, it is nearly impossible to get rid of them, even if that child—or child grown into an adult—wants to. The rote language wears a deep rut into our souls.

I can't single out my own church because the same sort of practice had been going on in one way or another for over fifteen hundred years in nearly all churches of the Western world. I certainly can't blame my parents or grandparents, either, because they were just doing what they had always done. But through my reflection on these matters, I saw my religious role in my heritage as breaking the pattern, at least for myself, that they could not. And so, I simply point out what was and what is and what it does to children.

The church begins this indoctrination early in a person's life. Like most of my church-going peers, I was in church every week, starting when I was a baby. As a result, these ritualistic, liturgical words became a foundation to my tiny faith. And the church and the pastor came to represent the mysterious God to me deep down in my unconscious psyche.

As a tyke, I didn't take too long to learn the words myself. I remember how proud I was the Sunday I stood up on the wooden pew next to my dad and, when the time came, with all the big people, I said the opening liturgy myself from memory. I was two, maybe three years old but then a big boy because I was reciting, "I confess that I am by nature sinful and unclean and cannot help myself." As I write this, I am once again stunned at the impact this would have on any small child who pays attention.

Were we really unclean by nature? Filthy creatures? I certainly don't think so now. But the idea of my guilt and worthlessness was planted and stuck with me in my God-concept. No wonder I was confused as an older child and thought God was something to keep at arm's length. I can't agree with Sigmund Freud on lots of things, but I can see why, during his years of research and practice, he was troubled by the church in Vienna and its practices that heaped guilt upon its members.

As I recognized what the church had done to me, at first I was angry, angry at religion. But I got over the anger by releasing it with forgiveness and by treating it as a grief issue. I am glad I was able to put the emotional part of the reaction behind me because holding onto the anger helped no one. It did not cause the church or any church or religion suddenly to change its ways and stop laying guilt upon its members. It only kept me small in my power and not fully effective. So when I released my anger, I actually freed myself from any control the indoctrination still had on me.

Of course, I reflected upon all of this as an adult. Children do not have the capacity to understand the psychological effects of such practices. They just hear the messages of the church, often delivered in the context of fear. Someone, somewhere got the wild idea it is a good thing to be afraid of God, to be scared. And I was. Then the churched added more, just to make me more fearful of God than I already was. Not that it took much. Imagine planting the horrific idea of burning in hell for all eternity in a little child's mind.

Church leaders must have thought that the worse they could scare kids into realizing both how rotten they were and how bad hell was, the better the good news of the gospel would sound. Trying to tell a kid that the good news is that God sent and sacrificed his own son to die a tortuous death on a cross to make up for our guilt didn't sound like very good news for that son. What kind of father does that? If God was a good father, he sure was funny about it, I mean weird. It also didn't make sense in my mind if that was how God kept his books about good and bad, right and wrong, reward and punishment. As a thoughtful kid, I would think about these things, and hardly any of it made any sense. But I was told to believe it, and so I did. It was Bishop Augustine, again, who said we should believe in order to understand, which is what my church advocated, as did others I knew about. But that theory doesn't make sense to a person who wants honesty in his or her religion. Not knowing any better, I obeyed and believed.

I can't truthfully tell anyone how much any of the people really understood the sermons, but whenever the ministers began to talk about hell, everyone listened. No one wanted to go there, and everyone wanted to know what the minimum good behavior was to escape hell. Going to heaven didn't sound good enough to make us want to do our best. What little we knew about it made it sound rather boring. But hell sounded horrific, and we had tremendous motivation to find out what to do to avoid going there. No one wanted eternal damnation—burning and burning and burning in hell without ever being burned up—that's how they described hell.

To top that off, they made Jesus the judge who decided who went to hell and who went to heaven, yet you were supposed to make your own personal decision. Worse, you only had one chance to get it right, and the one chance was what your entire life was for. I thought, why would it take an entire life? If someone made a decision, why not die right then and go to heaven? I had plenty of questions, but the church never had good answers.

We recited a creed every Sunday, the Apostles Creed, and we said, "I believe He will come again to judge the living and the dead." Jesus, apparently, had gone to heaven to wait and see how we did or what we believed, and he would return to judge us, sort us out, and send us to where we deserved to go. I envisioned a courtroom and Jesus up front in a black robe with a gavel. In hindsight, it sounds like rules a secular king would make up and then force his people to obey as a way to keep them in line.

So the devil and his hell really ruled us!

I want to share how the use of fear and guilt got so terrifying, and again, it came through the church. A guest pastor, an evangelist in the Norwegian tradition, was invited to hold special meetings, and the church was filled night after night to hear him speak. He was known as an expert preacher with the ability to wake people up and get them "really" saved (as if some were just saved and some were really saved), and his specialty was preaching on hell and the devil. People scooted to the edge of their seats when he reached the climactic moment in his sermon. Even though I was just a kid, I still remember it well. I know I couldn't take my eyes off him, and the entire church was so quiet I could have heard a pin drop. He raised his finger and shook it and pointed straight at me, so it seemed (although I later realized everyone thought he had pointed straight at each of them), and said "Hell!" when he brought down the wrath of God. It was as if the building shook.

Old timers said that the man "was really preaching the gospel, he sure was." Later, when I grew up, I learned the word "gospel" means "good news." Was this good news? Was this "really" preaching the gospel?

I might have thought I'd heard the gospel that evening, but I knew it didn't mean good news to me. When we got home in the dark that night, I was frightened more than I'd ever been. I can still feel my extreme fear, my terror. After I got to my room, I saw shadows moving across the wall from passing cars' lights, but they looked more like the devil dancing over my bed. Paralyzing fear held me in its grip. I was too scared to go to sleep because people died in bed and I could die that very night and I'd probably go to hell. At the same time, I wanted to go to sleep to escape the fright.

I later realized if I were to have a healthy relationship with God, which is a spiritual awareness of love, I would have to deal with these seeds planted in me early on. I knew I couldn't love God and be scared to death of him at the same time.

But for now, as I lay on my parents' couch and assessed the beliefs of my early life, I began to see the connection between the influence of my church and answers to questions now rising to the surface. If I were to find spiritual enlightenment, I would need to be clear on who I was and deal with these ideas the church had given me and which, yes, I had accepted. What was I made of? What was my essence? Uncleanness? Was I a sinner? Filthy and unclean? With no ability to do anything about it? Or was I a precious child of God, created in God's image? Was I good? Was I not a creature, after all, with a soul God could look at, in the eye, with loving companionship?

Was the devil a persona as powerful as God and someone who was out to get me?

Was Jesus the judge? How could he be a compassionate savior and friend if he were also my judge? Wouldn't only a weirdo be on trial in a courtroom and love the judge, as I was taught I should do? How could I possibly develop a loving relationship with Jesus and with God if I maintained the Jesus-as-judge belief?

After the wreck, I began my searching, and over time, my evaluation turned out well. I traveled from religion to reality, and I have not thrown out religion. How could I? It is massive. Humanity needs spiritual guidance. It always has and always will. We naturally seek it, and we can best fulfill this need by making sure our religions truly serve our innate desire to live a joyous life on Earth and help us find spiritual enlightenment, a higher consciousness free of guilt and fear.

I believe we are all on our best path at the moment, and all aspects of our life are serving us, directing us to go on or linger a bit or even turn around and try another route, as our journey unfolds. Job, career, family, neighborhood, city, health, choice of religion (or no religion), and more all play a part in our spiritual travels.

I still love the Lutheran religion. Why, when it added so much difficulty to my life, did I hold onto it? I believe that the Lutheran religious faith was brought into the world as a transition from the Middle Ages and, over the years, has done the best it could even though it only took us so far. And even after what I shared about my own bad experiences in my religion, I still loved religion—I loved the mystery, the prayers, the ancient writings, the purity of the chorals.

More important, the Lutheran religion connects me with my family and ancestors and heritage. My relatives brought this religion from Norway and Germany and passed it along to me. These people of the earth did not spend time questioning their faith or the doctrines of their religion; they focused on survival in the new land. I love them all. I visit their gravesites, think about them, the ones I know about, back to my great-great-grandparents, and feel a responsibility to stand on their shoulders, build on their lives, and move myself forward.

My ancestors landed at Ellis Island in New York, and made their way to the bitter winter cold of Wisconsin where they were assigned. Many died, but some found their way west. There, they lost land and crops in the Red River Valley when tornados destroyed everything, then loaded up what was left, and took a train to Seattle. They had heard about a valley that sounded like home in Norway, so they boarded a steamship going north to what became Bellingham and, by foot with their children, made their way twelve miles along an old Indian path through old-growth cedar to the Nooksak Valley, where they homesteaded. Their children populated the valley over the years, and when I, the fourth generation, grew up nearby, the family had grown so large that I ran into kids in school who were relatives I had never heard of.

The Lutheran Church for me is more than a religion. It connects me with my family, my heritage. My history lies in it, and I cannot separate if from me any more than I could sever my arm. It is one with me. Differences of opinion do not drive me away any more than an argument with a relative would send me away from my family.

Having said all of this, it does not mean I believe its messages and doctrines. What I continued to keep from my religion tied directly into how I saw myself, how I defined myself.

A powerful line in the movie, *Alice in Wonderland*, emphasizes this point. As Alice realizes she needs help to find her way, not only to survive but also to flee the land, she wonders, "Am I the *real* Alice?" Other characters question her, too: "Are you the real Alice?"

Then she meets the wise-old-man archetype and begs him for help. "Do you know who you are?" he asks (and I'm paraphrasing).

"I don't know who I am," she replies.

"I can't help you unless you know who you are," he tells her.

Wow. What a powerful statement.

Isn't that true of any of us? We can't find our purpose, and we can't approach our highest ability unless or until we discover who we really are.

The reflection I began back on my parents' couch eventually answered that basic question: Who am I? As I found ways along life to dump ineffective beliefs and build new and better ones, I discovered my true identity—not a creature sinful by nature but a clean and healthy human being, carved out of God's own nature. I thought about how kindly, compassionately, and lovingly powerful we all would be if we were to rid the world entirely of guilt feelings and the profiteering from guilt. Think of the increased clear energy we humans could have, making advances in health, science, and education; eradicating all hunger, sorrow, and disease; not to mention advancing the worlds of psychology, theology, philosophy, and all the social sciences. Imagine the ideas we would spark and the discoveries we would uncover. Would wars even be necessary? What if we all could come to know who we truly are—clean, wholesome, beautiful, and loving creatures—and see that our problems drop away when we honor our true nature.

After I began to examine my early beliefs and dig around in my psyche that had developed from those early religious indoctrinations, I realized that if I had to say which of us—Nancy or me—was closer to perfection, more prepared to move ahead into a new dimension with God, it was clearly Nancy. I was the one who needed to stay and work out my bad thinking. It was I who needed to remain behind; there was no question whatsoever that Nancy was the one in a better spiritual position to go on ahead with God.

By this time, it was late spring, more than six months since the accident. My body was healing, and my soul had begun the process too. I was ready for new challenges, new paths, new milieus in which to ponder my recent, self-exploratory thoughts.

My newly widowed friend Karen, who had visited me during the winter months, was perhaps on the right track: A Europe summer respite might be just the ticket to aid my healing and provide more answers.

I decided to go. Exploratory and adventurous by nature, I had sometimes gotten into jams I shouldn't have been in, and I doubted this trip would be any different. Maybe that would be a good thing, get me out of the norm and into thinking in new ways. After all, I was on a quest for different answers. And I loved excitement.

I located a bookstore, picked up the book, *Europe on $5 a Day*, bought my ticket on Icelandic Air, packed a few things, and boarded a train for the East Coast to catch the plane. One of my twin sisters, Suzanne, drove me to Vancouver, Canada, to ride the rails through the Canadian Rockies across Canada to Montreal, where I caught a bus for New York, and after a few days in the city, went out to JFK airport.

I had no idea who I'd meet, what experiences I'd have, and what spiritual lessons I'd learn. But it turned out to be more than I would have dreamed possible.

CHAPTER 4

As you enter a new phase of your existence, treat it
as if it were a game. It should be enjoyed not feared,
fun not work, played not endured, a reward rather
than a punishment.

Coach Lou Holtz
Notre Dame Football Coach

With a slight smile, I looked at my face in the little restroom mirror at the back of the Icelandic airplane. A week's worth of beard had sprouted since leaving by rail from Vancouver. Some was coming in a heavy black, and some was even grey, like my Welsh grandfather's rich mixture of grey and black hair but balanced with pure white when he was alive. The upper sides were blond, taking after my Norwegian side. Running my fingertips gently across my cheeks, I felt the soft little whiskers. Growing facial hair was bold for me, a rather traditional guy, and represented a new adventure. After the weight of grief upon me over the past six months, I was determined to enjoy Europe and the Middle East and make the trip fun. Somehow, growing a beard connected having fun with entering a new phase of my life, and I wanted to start it with a bold yet enjoyable healing first step. As much as I expected to meet interesting people and encounter exciting experiences, I also hoped to gain insight to the purpose of my life, especially in relation to my spiritual search.

We touched down smoothly on the landing strip at the Luxembourg airport on that warm and sunny June afternoon, and I could feel a stir of emotion bouncing around the cabin. Within minutes, I was lingering on the ramp's top step about twenty feet above the tarmac and pulling a full breath of European air into my lungs. I felt exhilarated, even rather romantic and excited. This bright summer would be a vacation away from grief and sorrow, so I hoped. But I knew it offered more. In my thoughts, I would probe into the newly formed crevasses in my heart that the sudden tragedy had created, and I would try to make sense of it.

In fact, one burning question was emerging, a residue of unfinished business, and as the summer progressed, I thought about it more and more from all angles. Why? *Why*? Why did that wreck happen and kill Nancy and destroy my new marriage? And when I got to the core of this question, it became a God question: If God was a good God, and if God was all-powerful and could have prevented that highway crash, then why didn't he? If he could have caused the difference of a split second between Nancy and me and the other car, and obviously, God didn't, why was that? Why didn't God step in? Wasn't God in control? Why didn't I understand? Didn't God understand? What went wrong? How could I explain this to myself in a way that gave me peace so I could stop torturing myself with this question? And just as important, how could my concept of God at this point fit into the reality?

I had no good answers, and no one who had tried to help me had done any better. Since Nancy's death, some people had shared Bible verses with me to comfort me. They would say things like, "Terry, all things work for good. That's what the Bible says." They were implying I should not let the question bother me. Just sit back and be passive. When I analyzed the Bible, however, I found that was not what the passage from Paul was about in its original context (Romans 8:28 "We know that in everything God works for good with those who love him, who are called according to his purpose"), but their answer was tempting because of its simplicity. Further thinking with even a little commonsense, though, showed the shallowness of their interpretation and made no sense, common or otherwise.

Another said God was testing me. My mind couldn't accept that either. I thought, if this is about a test, it is a downright rotten test—to let someone wonderful, whom everyone loved, who had a bright future and a great faith, be killed in such a wicked manner, slaughtered, out on the highway, as Nancy was. And to cause severe human heartbreaks for family and friends. Killing her to test me? That didn't even happen to the Biblical Isaac who was tied to an altar, ready for a sacrifice that God called off. Or if we can't take the idea of God doing the killing, wording it differently suggested the same thing—that God let her be killed. He allowed it. No, I thought. Those who suggest that this was a test from God should lay their head on my pillow of recovery. Battle my nightmares of headlights racing at me night after night. Hear the weeping, running through loved ones. Stand in my shoes. Feel Nancy's dream for lover, home, and family snuffed out in an instant. No, trite answers would not suffice.

But if I couldn't answer a simple, one-word question like *why*, then what kind of religion did I have, anyway?

Some well-intentioned religious people felt they had the answer. They told me in letters or conversations that the devil had killed Nancy. Their explanation did no better in answering the question (so why did the devil kill her?), and it only gave me weird feelings. That horrible fear of the devil I had had as a kid was gone now because I had realized God is bigger than any devil we can manufacture. But I began to feel some Christians were in danger of putting the devil up on a pedestal, on an equal power with God, as if the devil could do something to us when God wasn't watching and get away with it. These people seemed to have two gods—a good god, the Christian God, and an evil god, his enemy, the devil. They were portrayed as two gods on equal footing. That wouldn't wash. Something did not ring true to me about that back then. I had always been taught that the ultimate God was one and only one, and I didn't see then and don't see now why that needs to be any different.

Blaming the devil reminded me of Flip Wilson-type theology. Flip Wilson had a variety show on television, and he gave a standard line, "The devil made me do it," whenever he did something wrong. It gave him a convenient excuse for any mistake and always brought the house down with laughs. People liked it and related to putting the blame on someone else.

Along this line, one man who I barely knew had driven hundreds of miles just to see me in the hospital in Georgia and tell me that the devil did it. I remember the brief visit well. I was in my hospital bed and couldn't move, trapped in all sorts of hardware and pulleys connected to my chest, arms, and legs. He came in, sat down uninvited on the chair by the bed, and opened his Bible and read. His voice and hands were shaking, and he told me the devil had done this. "That's all I came to say." And he stood up and left. No condolences. No conversation. No questions to discuss.

To be fair, most people did share condolences and didn't try to figure out the why of it and push on me their convictions. But for some people, giving me an explanation was important to them.

Still, all of these encounters gave me reasons to delve beyond the obvious or commonly accepted advice. The big question of *why* and others' answers to that question and my own grappling with the issues gave me plenty to reflect on that summer as I journeyed through Europe and even as far as Israel.

I had the idea I wanted to visit small villages and be able to be independent in my travels, so I had found a shop in Luxembourg back when I first landed and purchased a motor scooter, of all things. Soon I was making my way through the German countryside, stopping at various sites and visiting war memorials as I headed towards Berlin. But I couldn't follow the most direct or fastest route. Once I got the scooter on the road, it topped out at probably thirty miles per hour, so I definitely kept off the autobahn. Taking the slower route let my mind wander in keeping with the easier pace and put me in touch with people and experiences I probably would not have found on the major expressway. For instance, one time when I stopped in a small village to spend the night, I found the local place to stay—a quaint little three- or four-room hotel, just what I was looking for. It turned out to be a farm with the rooms upstairs and the cattle below. The lavatory consisted of a cute little wooden room down the hall and had a seat with a hole in it that dropped all the way down, two stories, to the ground-floor hole in the earth below. I was getting acculturated—at least to the countryside.

Riding through the open country, my thoughts on why began to run deeper. As I traveled, I thought if the devil could take a life, if he had that type of power, then where was God? I surmised that if God was still all-powerful, the devil could not have killed Nancy without God's permission … which made God a part of it. God would be guilty and culpable. At the very least, then God was weak, not omnipotent.

But to top it off, I was a Christian, and so was Nancy. We were members of the church. We believed in God and Jesus. We believed Jesus was all-powerful. And our religion taught that as believers, we were saved and as Christians, we had special protection. God looked after us more than he did others with Jesus and angels watching over us. So what went wrong? Ultimately, these questions would jar my faith, and rightly so.

Of course, there was the common, simple, and earthly answer we could all grasp, one that had little to do with God and, for that reason, carried huge implications and certainly did not fit into the beliefs of our religion at the time. It went like this: A guy was negligibly speeding as he checked out how fast his car could go; the pavement was slick; he lost control and crossed the freeway to smash head-on into us. It was an accident. We were in the wrong place at the wrong time, and we happened to collide. One person was killed. Really too bad. That's all there was to it. It was simply an unfortunate accident. Nothing more. Things happen. God had nothing to do with it. As the song goes that Doris Day made famous, "*Que sera, que sera* (whatever will be, will be)." But that would seem to take away any protection from God we believed we had. And it was a theology too, when I thought about it, and it had the potential to make us passive people.

I thought of Nancy many times and knew she would have wanted to be with me, pondering these things, too. As I lay in my hotel room in Germany one evening, I remembered her words, Georgia accent and all, "Oh, Terry, I can hardly wait." I saw again in my mind her velvet blue eyes as I did whenever I thought of her. But that night, my mind turned them from a twinkling smile to a hauntingly serious gaze. I wasn't sure what she was seeing then as she looked at me, but I knew I was feeling a glory and thrill about life beyond what I had known was possible. But, then, after the few minutes for that visit in my memory and feeling renewed exhilaration, I realized where I was and felt an emptiness move across my stomach once again. Such changes from moments of supreme happiness to feelings of utter grief were not unusual that summer.

The more I thought about it, the question of why this happened in relationship to God seemed to have the potential to drive me mad. None of the proposed answers made sense. I didn't want *why* in the back of my mind all the time, and I didn't want to spoil this trip and the adventure opening a new chapter in my life. So still early in my travels in Europe, perhaps within the first month, I decided to let the question go for the time and enjoy the trip.

That summer's travel exposed me to different ways of living and opened my mind to people of other nationalities, cultures, and religions, and that, in turn, prepared me to open up to the Spirit in a broader way even through other religions later. As I saw practices different from my own that worked for others, I questioned the idea that the Western way was the best way. And that carried over into wondering about the validity of religious beliefs I had been taught. How could some people be so good who weren't Christian in the way I thought of being a Christian?

I was also aware of my search for the purpose I felt I had ahead for me, and I learned later that I was doing the best thing. Getting to the spiritual awareness I was looking for would require an openness to different ideas, and starting with being open to others, to their lifestyles, their cultures, and their religions, would prepare the way for reexamining my own tightly held beliefs. Encounters with people of different beliefs and values that summer did feed into my experience and the process that paved the path of what I was searching for and would find much later. It opened the door to broader thinking just a crack—but open enough later, much later, to let the door fly wide open.

After a wonderful week exploring Rome, another pondering Athens and other parts of Greece, and then one more in Turkey where much of the New Testament took place, I arrived at my farthest destination, Israel. As my ship docked in Haifa, a long-anticipated dream was right at my feet.

I had already traveled the land of Israel and walked the dusty roads and trails in my imagination because it was the Bible Land, and I had been fascinated with maps for many years as I read the stories. But what a joy, now, to reach down and pick up a palm full of soil of the Holy Land and let it trickle through my fingers and, later, to meet fishermen on Galilee and go out on the water overnight and, then later, to meditate on the hillside where Jesus supposedly gave the Sermon on the Mount.

Then one day in Jerusalem, I noticed a billboard advertising a five-day camping adventure trip, touring the Sinai Desert. I stood facing the flier and read it over and over. Wow! That's for me! I decided, knowing this was only a year after one of the great wars in the region. Nonetheless, I liked camping, I liked exploration, and not many modern people had ever traveled through that historic, lonely Sinai Desert. We have nothing like it in America.

Wearing cut-off shorts and a T-shirt the entire five days, along with a red handkerchief bandana I tied over my hair, I joined twenty-seven other adventurers, almost all Israeli Jews, riding along the sandy roads in open-air jeeps, called command cars. The wind began catching my budding beard and hair as we flew along the first day across the northern Sinai to the Suez Canal.

Our caravan included a family with their kids, a few couples, and the rest either partners and friends or a few singles, like me. With about equal numbers of men and women, the group had no one older than about sixty, probably because the flier said it was a rugged trip. Many times, we drove and rode where little to no road lay before us, and when it did, it was usually mere tire tracks in the sand.

We also drove with the possibility of death hanging over us. Although the area had been mined during the war and the military had tried to clear all the mines, we knew some remained. These trips ran every two weeks, and on the previous trip, one of the trailers with the gear, behind the command cars, with its narrower axle hit a mine that had not been removed, blew up, and sent shrapnel everywhere, killing a man riding in the back seat. Everyone knew about the explosion, and no one wanted that back seat. I didn't fight for a seat any morning, and feeling like nothing worse could happen to me now, I was comfortably riding in the back seat the entire trip. I had it to myself, felt safe, and we struck no mines.

The drivers, all men in their twenties and thirties who had fought in the war, were vested in teaching us how they had won. We slept in the open and, because it was warm, on top of sleeping bags until we got up to a higher elevation. I delighted in this chance to see stars as I had never seen them before. From one side of the desert floor to another, the entire sky sang with enlightened, sparkling glory. Oh my, just to think about it now… a mass of white constellations pouring over the firmament. I did not want to close my eyes.

The company had stocked our food supply from a warehouse of wartime military rations in tins. If we wanted hot meals, we had to gather wood or brush, build a fire, and cook them over open fires. It was definitely a camping trip, but I loved it, even with meals nothing like the delightful ones I had been having—pastas of Italy coated with rich sauces and lamb chops of Greece oozing with rich virgin olive oil and spices and herbs.

In my open command car, I had the pleasure of two fun-loving girls—art students from France—and we got to know each other. Not much younger than I, they were full of excitement, joy, and laughter, and bubbled over with enthusiasm, as well as curiosity. I didn't know what to expect of art students, but they proved to be delightful. Anyone would have found both of them especially attractive—in their tight jeans and light tops, as the fashion styles and the temperature dictated at the time.

"Here, Terry, it's your turn," the shorter one said as she handed me a military tin. In her other hand, she held her own and settled down on a little desert log in the sand next to me that first evening at the Suez Canal.

The attention felt special, and her presence only made me miss Nancy more. But it did feel nice. I assumed they came from the Mediterranean side of France, the southern area, because they both had lighter olive complexions and dark hair. The young woman sitting next to me had a face that belonged on the cover of a fashion magazine—a beautiful shape and alert, sparkling, dark brown eyes. She was the one who did the most for me—with a bit of light-hearted banter thrown in for fun.

The three of us enjoyed ourselves. The girls seemed to compete in a good-natured way to wait on me, and I enjoyed it. In return, I built fires in the sand with brush I gathered, which I knew how to do from hiking trips back in the Cascade Mountains of Washington State, and the girls cooked the food—well, opened the old military tins and warmed them up over the fire.

"So, tell me, you're from France?" I said in English as we tried to believe the rations tasted good.

"Oh, yes, but isn't it exciting to be *here*?" the attentive one said as she stretched her legs flat over the sand to hold her military rations.

I love foreign accents, and I think French is one of the most enticing.

"I love it. I like hot weather. I like the sunshine. I like the bit of danger we are in," I said, making small talk.

"We do too—*oui*," she said, "but I didn't know of any danger. *Parlez-vous français*, Terry?"

"*Non. Un peu*," I said. Only a little.

"Good, because we want to practice English. Will you help?"

"*Oui*," I said. I lamely added a little more in French that I remembered from high school before switching to English for them

"So you're making a summer vacation in Israel?" I asked.

"Oh, we are college girls, and we're Jews, and this is something we want to do."

"I see. College in France?"

"*Oui*, we are both art students."

Serious conversation wasn't our thing right then, or even any other time the entire trip—just a lot of fun and curiosity and even some playing around in the sand around camp in the evenings. We acted like little children at the beach—dancing in the sand, running and hiding, exploring little areas near camp. Sometimes, we just sat and talked by the campfire—or on the beach on those couple of nights when we were next to the water. Other tour participants were with families or friends, so the three of us made a natural little family group of our own.

I pondered, though, as I sat in the back of that open-air command car, about how that land was a crossroads. Three major religions trace their history to that area and claim the land as theirs. Does anything create barriers, hatreds, murders, and wars between people more than religion? The Christians and Moslems had had their wars nearly a thousand years ago, and now the Moslems and Jews had been having theirs. When will it end, I wondered, and then I let the wind carry such thoughts away.

We made it to the heart and center of the desert, to the foot of Mt. Sinai. It was also the objective of the trip, and a climb to the top the next day was planned. Its rocky grandeur loomed before us and rose right up out of the sandy desert floor, waiting for our ascent. At the base, rested the glorious, ancient Saint Catherine's Monastery, some sixteen hundred years old.

That night, we slept in a little camp in our sleeping bags on the sand. In my imagination, I heard the stars serenading us, and with my eyes, I saw them in the purest of clear, desert air, sparkling brighter than ever before. It was a show of nature and the universe and created an awe-inspiring mood to fit the deep connection I felt to the Holy Land.

Those of us who answered the three o'clock musical call from one of the leaders rose from our warm bags to begin the climb in the dark to the top of Mt Sinai. The French girls and I were bringing up the rear and whispered softly along the trail as we started up the mountain by flashlight. It was pitch black, but when I raised my head, I could see other flashlights from people ahead. Speaking quietly—or not at all—felt more respectful. The trail was actually steps for much of the path, steps worn deeply in the rock mountain by centuries of pilgrims making this same ascent. I could never figure out how a human foot could cause rock to wear away, but it does, given enough feet and enough centuries. By that time of the night, I noticed the stars did not give much light, and the near full moon following the sun was long gone, down behind other mountains to the west.

I chuckled to myself at how scared the girls were. "What is there to be afraid of?" I asked.

"Maybe there are snakes or wild animals," one said. "We don't know."

"We've never done anything like this before," the other said. Indeed, many of our group—I didn't count—remained behind and never made the climb. Some opted out because of fear of the mountain, I learned.

The girls stayed close to me and held on to my hands and arms as we wound up the steep trail. One held onto my belt sometimes, and I realized that wilderness hiking was not in their history.

"Terry, what do you know about this place?" they asked, as just a peek of light began to spread from the east.

What did I know about this place? More than they did, interestingly enough. The young Jewish women didn't know too much about their own history, that the Ten Commandments are reputed to have come directly from God at the top of this mountain, for example. Interestingly, neither the drivers nor any of our group said anything about Moses when we were there. Even the girls didn't know much about them so I filled them in.

And then I added to the better-known facts about the Ten Commandments something I had learned earlier in my studies.

"There is one thing I do know that might interest you and that they did not tell us on the tour. In fact, I don't think they even know about it," I said, now speaking in a normal tone. We weren't climbing fast, and people ahead slowed us down, so no one was out of breath. We really had to watch the steep trail, though, but chattering was impossible not to do.

"What did he not tell us?" they asked.

"I had a teacher once, back in the USA, who loved history as a hobby, who was quite excited about this place. He told me about the monastery."

One of the Greek monks had given us a tour of parts of the monastery the night before after we had arrived and set up camp.

"My teacher said there were ancient manuscripts hidden here, a lot of them, and no outsider has seen them yet," I said. "I think they are buried away in a secret, inner room they discovered when they tore down some walls and were remodeling in the 1950s."

"Is there no way we can see them?"

"No, the most valuable manuscript they ever had was removed and taken away from them in the nineteenth century by foreign scholars, and the monks still feel they were robbed. So they don't trust outsiders and won't share any more of their finds. It is really tragic, though, because they do not have the expertise to know what they have. I saw that one manuscript in the British Museum."

I did not know it then, but that early Greek manuscript became accepted as one of the most accurate of all the known written artifacts from this region. I agree and now use it when I translate the Bible from its original Greek.

We climbed the last little narrow incline and stepped up to the summit—a small rocky crag—at just about daylight. The golden sun was just following the radiant pinks and oranges we had been climbing by, and we were fortunate enough to see the head of the sun begin to pop up once we got to the top. It revealed innumerable other rugged cliffs spread out across the desert. And each second, as the sun slowly rose, showed us another breathtaking panoramic view. Glancing down, I spotted a herd of Bedouin sheep, thousands of feet below, meandering along centuries-old trails embedded in the desert floor.

Then more orange streaks shot streams of sunlight across the tops of the other rocky crags below us, followed by a full sun out across the horizon. I have never seen anything like it, before or since.

By now, other people in our group on that little peak were chattering away, but I was quiet and not paying them any attention.

Here, I thought, this famous site holds the legend of the Ten Commandments. Not that they are so different from other ancient laws of other cultures, but I reveled in the feeling of being at the actual place where something I'd heard about my entire life had happened.

All too soon, we carefully made our steps back down the mountain, packed up, and were on our way.

That night we made it to a large oasis on the Red Sea, our most beautiful camping location of the entire trip, so perfect a setting, it could have been in a movie. Palm trees surrounded a small fresh water lake, perfectly still when we arrived, and reflected the bright blue sky. Lush greenery contrasted with the bordering dry desert and refreshed the eyes as well as the other senses with its hints of moistness. This peaceful, magical place had been a common overnight stop for Bedouins for centuries, if not millenniums.

But I couldn't appreciate the beauty when we first arrived. Instead, I felt I had to get away. I had been thinking about the *why* question again—why the accident, why Nancy's death, why the whole tragedy. And this time, I didn't shove it aside. I now felt I had to confront it in some meaningful way, and that desire superseded any thoughts of our beautiful surroundings.

Something was rumbling inside me, calling me to get outside the circle and go in the direction of a nearby, tall sand dune. It stood behind us, maybe one-hundred-fifty-feet- or two-hundred-feet-high and one or two hundred yards to the west. The air was so clear it was not easy to measure distance by eye.

I left camp and walked through the greenery around to the south, following a tiny path in the sand, to find a little valley behind the dune. I put my feet in the sand and managed to climb to the top. Our camp spread out before me, and I could see people building little campfires to cook their dinner. Just behind the camp and oasis lay the beautifully blue Red Sea. Behind me, the sun was about to drop, and once it did, there would be no twilight, no in-between time, waiting for darkness to fall.

What follows is a deeply personal part of the trip and a very important part of my journey towards spiritual awakening.

I began to release my emotions out loud and talk to God, believing if he couldn't or wouldn't listen, at least I was venting to myself.

The camp was so far away no one would hear me. And I got loud, but not shouting loud.

Then it fell completely dark, but I was very comfortable sitting there in the sand, and a full moon rose before long. It was a pinkish orange color at first and as large as you can imagine, looking close enough that you could reach out and touch it.

"Okay, God," I said, "I get it." I felt the rumbling inside me begin to take shape and spill out in a kind of a prayer experience.

"I can't live a sane life if I keep asking you this question, and my mind wouldn't be able to understand the answer you might give, anyway. I'm through asking you *why*."

This was a breakthrough moment.

"My three pounds of brain can't put together anything that makes any sense to me right now. I know in my head you are larger than anything, than even a universe, and I don't think your answer to my question would make sense to me. That's what I've concluded. That must be why I can't figure it out."

My subconscious seemed to take over my thoughts, and I heard myself saying the words that effortlessly flowed out.

"I guess it is something that only your mind, greater than mine, has reserved for you. Maybe, it is not an important question to you— but I can't believe that. Maybe one day, it won't matter to me—the question, I mean. Maybe one day, I'll move closer to your reality and understand what you understand. Maybe one day, the answer will just pop into my head. Or maybe, you don't have an answer.

"But for now," I said, "in terms of the answer … whatever I sense you have to say, I'll accept. If you say nothing, I'll accept that, too. The pain is just too high for me to keep asking. So, for now, I give up.

"I'm leaving this question to you, the great God, and I will try to find out what I should do."

While I didn't realize the impact of that new thought at the time, I had stumbled onto a question I could answer—"What can I do about this?" I had replaced *why* with *what*, not *why* did this happen, but *what* can I do about it?

It was dark now except for the full moon continuing to rise in the east. A cool breeze began to slip by off the water. Before long, I stood up, feeling much better, and made my way down through the soft sand on the backside of the sand dune in the dark and found my way to camp. Dinner was gone, and I wasn't hungry. Others were gathered around campfires, but I made my way alone to my sleeping bag. I nestled on it and was soon fast asleep and slept peacefully.

What should I do with my life, now became my focus, not why did this happen. Instead of looking back for an *intellectual* answer, I began to look ahead for a *practical* answer. I now knew I needed to answer how I could contribute to turn this horrifying tragedy into something good for somebody.

The early twentieth-century theologian Alfred North Whitehead said, "The kingdom of heaven is not the isolation of good from evil. It is the overcoming of evil by good." That is what I was going to try to do, even through all the pain so many were suffering. I could not bring Nancy back into the world, and grieving forever when healing was available would be entirely selfish. I realized I wanted to find some way to turn the evil into a positive for many in the world, and that doing so would be a victory.

On that evening and on that dune, I got the start of the great answer. Maybe one day, I will get to go there again and remember, but I doubt it. It belongs to Egypt now. I had let the burning question go because it was unanswerable and replaced it with a better question. Knowing *why* wouldn't help anyone. But getting involved in seeing what pieces I could pick up and care for would. It no longer mattered to me if the tragedy was caused by the devil or God, or if it was just an accident, or about why it happened. It just ... was. For now, I had given it over to God.

And now, if I still believed God was good and that he was a God of love—and I did, at least in my head—*what* could I do next? I was ready to explore the possibilities. I knew drifting into bitterness wouldn't help anyone, not at all. Who cared? Bitterness simply had the potential to ruin at least one life in particular, mine, so I didn't want to go there. What good could I now get into? I didn't know, but my antennas were up. I had a lot to learn, more than a lot and more than I realized, before I would finally understand my purpose. Lessons learned the hard way still awaited me.

My trip wasn't over. In fact, the greatest discoveries were yet to come, spiritual discoveries that helped change my life and change my thinking more deeply.

CHAPTER 5

I enter in the game of living with joyful anticipation,
with enthusiasm.

Ernest Holmes
Author

My encounters with unnecessary human suffering in this chapter played vital and essential roles in the unfolding spiritual path before me because they opened me up to feeling a broader sense of compassion. Each experience turned out to lead deeper into my unique passageway towards higher consciousness and enlightenment. At the time, I did not understand how suffering could aid in my journey. But eventually, I realized that spiritual consciousness is not some sort of flying up into outer space; but that genuine spirituality includes awareness of all life and all aspects of life.

The Sinai trip had been an experience of a lifetime. As we parted ways, my new French student friends and I said our goodbyes with wishes for continuing success.

Getting around Israel for a final view was not difficult. Once in a while, like the day I went to Hebron to see the three-thousand-year-old grave-cave of Abraham, I rode a bus, where some of the passengers held a cage or two of chickens cackling away. Other times, I simply hooked up with someone I met at a hostel or restaurant and got a ride. At night, for the most part, with the warm weather, I found a tree to sleep under, using my sleeping bag for padding. It was safe, and I loved the adventure, dealing with the unexpected. Each day brought something new, and being with people of a new culture and a different language enlivened my travels.

One of my fortuitous meetings put me in touch with two German students. They were going to explore, as I was, the famous Masada. Originally created by Herod, one-time king of the Jews, as a safe retreat for himself, this mountain-top rock fortress bordering the Dead Sea later was used as a secure place for nearly one thousand Jews to hold out against the Roman invasion of Palestine in the late first century.

What I knew of the place had sparked my interest to see Masada in person and to understand the courage and feelings of those who had lived there in exile and to grasp the cruelty of the Roman Tenth Legion. Readings and lectures convey only so much; I wanted to immerse myself and all my senses in it and, somehow, connect to the occupants of thousands of years ago. I was attempting to understand human nature from experience, not only the university, and the path to authentic spirituality. I had learned that when the tough Roman Tenth Legion pushed its way through Israel in the year 70 CE, it leveled Jerusalem and executed Jews or sent them to Rome as slaves. That was how they enforced the pax Romana, the thousand-year peace of Rome. Nearly one thousand Jews escaped the carnage and made their way through the wilderness to Masada (which means fortress), which became a secure refuge for them for nearly three years.

The German couple and I decided to hook up and, together, find our way out into the wilderness to Masada. We had no way to get there, no public transportation, and we weren't sure exactly where it was anyway. But outside Beersheba, we hitched a ride on the back of an Israeli farmer's old flatbed truck, and he took us on the ride of a lifetime. Riding in low gear, we slowly dropped down to the east over the edge of the sheer canyon wall to the Dead Sea in Israel's southwest, eleven hundred feet below sea level, the lowest valley on earth. The kind farmer dropped us off where a little dirt road spilled out from the mountains to the west to meet the paved road we had been driving on, running north and south. He pointed us up that little dirt road, and we could see that it headed up to the base of a cliff where entered the foot of the famous switchback Snake Path trail, leading to the top of Masada.

Little vegetation marked the desert there next to the Dead Sea as we walked up to and alongside two-thousand-year-old Roman encampments, still marked in place with rock fencing. However, about four hundred feet above, the fortress plateau remained hidden from our view. I understand now how its location had been lost for nearly two thousand years, rediscovered only in 1838 by two American archaeologists.

Once we found the Snake Path, we began our climb. Ascending switchback by switchback, twisting and turning, I quickly learned how the trail got its name. One step after another, we made the climb, and it wasn't too bad. Still early in the day and not as hot as it would become later, I even felt energized. In pauses along our way, we referenced facts in my *Europe on $5 a Day*, which I carried in my pack.

Reaching the top with a little sweat dripping down, I turned to the east and looked out over the Dead Sea as Herod might have done, standing at his stone railing, and I felt incredibly free. I noticed the quietness, the feeling of peace. And yet it felt an odd peace, incomplete perhaps and not a happy one, surely mixed with the story in the back of my mind about the nine hundred ninety-six suicides.

The guidebook directed us around the eighteen acres and explained the story in detail. Although Jews had escaped to Masada, the Romans eventually discovered their hiding and, over nearly three years, built a land bridge from the nearest mountain. The night before the onslaught was to begin, the Jews knew their time had come as the Romans partied in anticipation of long-awaited spoils the next day—raping women, torturing some to a slow, painful death, grabbing whatever booty they could find as souvenirs, taking some children to Rome in cages for a victory parade and then turning them into lifetime slaves.

But the Jews had another idea to cheat the victor of spoils. They carefully prepared a deadly poison, first giving it to the children, then to themselves, and robbed the merciless Tenth Legion of its pent-up anger and anticipated delight.

Upon excavation, archaeologists found graves of women and children that the Romans had missed and left some for all to see as a memorial. Open reminders of death, preserved in the desert climate for centuries, chilled my soul. I saw one woman's skull with only a little hair remaining and realized that the army had simply chopped off her hair.

Standing there where the Romans finally broke through from the north, I can't describe my feelings well. They were outlandish to me, so bright to see and too hot to handle, if this makes any sense. I just know something had changed inside of me. I was different. I wanted to weep for those who had died here, yet I was proud of them.

As I stood on that high ground now with a bit of a warm breeze flowing behind me from the sea to the east, my earlier peacefulness turned into a mountain of pain. Through what I experienced by casting myself back into their experience, I also felt the torture of humans everywhere in the world. My heart was opened to human suffering in a new way, and I would look to find the source. What were we doing wrong? Where was—and is—compassion in our world? Is it true most of us think of ourselves first, me too? Are some people truly so hardened to other humans they can slaughter mercilessly? Are these people part of the same human race? I knew from working through issues from my childhood that telling people they are wicked or sinful and unclean does not help. It puts them into a defensive, hardened posture, and they lash out. So what do we do to grow out of violent behavior?

The questions remained unanswered as I left the fortress, and they lingered in the back of my mind as I continued my travels. I do not think climbing Masada before I left Israel was an accident. I needed that experience to prepare me for later steps on my spiritual journey, to understand human suffering—of others and not just my own—before I could find the way to move into the consciousness of joy

Thanks to my sister Suzanne, I continued my travels after Israel with a final trip with a Eurail Pass that could be purchased only in the United States. I was able to go through Europe to places I had not seen in my earlier travels. I enjoyed unlimited first-class train travel and spent a relaxing time at wonderful places, including the art-drenched cities of Florence and Venice, the playful French Rivera, and Scandinavia, home to my ancestors.

However, my visit to the Dachau WWII concentration camp in Munich, Germany, made a far more powerful impression. Dachau, the first Nazi concentration camp, through which over two hundred thousand marched, and the second concentration camp the Americans liberated at the end of the war, stands in a suburb on the outskirts of Munich. Crowning the top of the wide gate at the entrance, a metal engraving reads, "*Arbeit macht frei*," meaning, "through work one will be free." I was not sure if that referred to the former munitions factory on the site or was actually put in place for the concentration camp itself.

The simplicity of the entrance belies the turmoil most experience who visit the site. Reminders within the compound of the horrors that some inflicted and others suffered at their hands cannot fail to affect all who pass through, and I among them. Dachau yanked at my heartstrings, touching me deeply.

Until entering the gate of Dachau, I had had only an academic understanding of the word "holocaust." It was a word in my head, like a word in the dictionary or something to read about in a college textbook rather than a word in my heart connected to a personal experience or empathy for others. In other words, I had taken in only the facts—that untold numbers of people had been slaughtered in cold blood in these concentration camps because of who they were—and I had not let myself feel anything about those facts. Now, walking the grounds, stepping inside the buildings, seeing the living quarters connected me with what those in Dachau had experienced and permanently changed my life.

Spending hours roaming the massive Dachau complex, I let my heart soften and my consciousness expand as I opened myself to my feelings. I had moved well beyond an academic exercise. Tears wetted my eyes. Deep grief—pain and sorrow—flooded over me. I identified with those victims. People who loved one another, whose lives revolved around each other, who depended upon another were torn apart. Boys were separated from their mothers, children from their siblings, spouses sent to two lines, never to see one another again. What had the Nazis done?

At the entrance to the camp, a war memorial museum told the story, complete with graphic photos. Outside, I was free to roam through a reconstructed living building to walk into, touch, feel, and experience the life they had lived. On this one warm, summer day, I imagined how, day after day of the bitter cold winter, they had faced inhumane living that, for many, ended only in execution.

I found myself weeping, almost embarrassingly so, until I noticed others around me in stark quietness, almost silence, also sobbing. My grief of the loss of my own wife was reaching up and touching me at this moment also. I remember one young man in particular, who wore a little cap and looked to be in his twenties, seated off to the side, quietly crying. How could something so tragic happen in this world? Weren't we all humans? Even the Nazis? Of course, I knew the answer in my head, as did everyone else, but I was only just learning to think with my heart about the true reasons behind the Holocaust and other tragedies of injustice.

Reports are that on occasion, guards herded a group of people to the firing range and used them for target practice while they smoked cigars and laughed.

In my mind's eye, I saw people rising to life and standing in rows before me, people in line for the execution of Hitler's "final solution," which was extermination. I experienced people forced to disrobe for the "showers," and I myself stood under those same shower heads, the better to imagine and ponder. Not one of the few people outside walking the grounds wanted to walk into the shower rooms, so I walked through slowly and alone. I assumed it was too harsh of a reality for some, to walk through as the prisoners had to their death.

The Nazis forced the people take off all their clothes, leaving them outside the shower room, and then herded them in mass into a large room with shower heads hanging from the ceiling. After bolting the doors shut, the Nazis stepped onto the roof and dropped death pellets down into fake shower heads. When the pellets hit bottom, they released a killer gas that spread out into the room, and soon everyone was lying dead. The Nazis quickly came through with hammers, jarred open every mouth, and knocked out gold teeth to help pay for the war. I got as much reality as I could stand when I looked up straight into the tiny holes of those rusting old shower heads on the ceiling. In my imagination, I heard the tap, tap, tap as guards dropped pills in from above. I even imagined guards chuckling as they dropped the pills, which reports indicate they did, before rushing down to strip the bodies of gold. I stood there and listened with my imagination and heard screams as naked people began falling.

Feeling every disconsolate emotion within me, I then walked outside from the shower rooms a short distance and sat in front of the old red brick building, its outdoor furnaces now somewhat deteriorating. I imagined one body after another rising up through the chimney in smoke after it was thrown into the furnace. Reports also indicate that the Nazis forced some Jews to perform this distasteful task, tossing the dead bodies of their own into the fires.

My heart ached. I wanted no one else to go through these kinds of things, ever again.

But my response went beyond my tear-filled eyes and inner sobbings and feelings of utter compassion for all who had suffered there. As awful as I felt, I determined not to get caught in the academic and intellectual trap of asking why too much but concentrated on what we can do, going forward, to put an end to this kind of painful nonsense on earth. It connected with my replacing *why* with *what do I do* and my search for a purpose that would count in the world and help others seeking a meaningful spiritual life for themselves, which must surely stop such horrors of human against human. Not that I had an answer, but I recognized that this process—the experience of relating to those in the concentration camp—was part of discovering the greater path in my life.

I pocketed that experience, knowing it would contribute somehow to my spiritual journey and without my constantly thinking about it, which I could not do, not without going crazy. I could absorb only so much pain at once.

I toured other parts of Munich and then continued on, eventually winding up in Barcelona, Spain. There I had an incredible, spiritual experience that to this day sends chills through me.

Before debarking from the train in Barcelona, I consulted my *Europe on $5 a Day* to check out the map and sites I'd want to visit in this city of almost two million. Eager to get going, and figuring it would be easy to get a room for the night later as I had in other cities, especially as it was September and past the height of tourist season, I spent the day sightseeing. I would have one more day in the city before catching the speed train in the evening for Paris, where my friend Karen was waiting to see me.

Toward evening, I began my search for a small room that night, using Barcelona's strange but interesting custom for seeking accommodations: Room seekers walked into a block and clapped their hands three times to attract a hotel or inn doorkeeper. Someone, invariably a historic-looking little bent-over man in dark garb, would pop out from the shadows with a huge ring of old keys—one for every door on his block. Block after block I tried this. I walked on and clapped my hands. The key keepers came to me, always, but I found no room available. "No," I heard block after block.

No matter, it was only eight o'clock. But evening wore into late evening, and late evening wore close into the bewitching midnight hour. No one was left on the streets now, and I was still walking and clapping, moving farther and farther from the city. The old key keepers were still coming from the shadows.

"*Salle, por favor,*" was my standard line by now. (Do you have a room?) Again, no.

My Spanish was non-existent for the most part. And no one spoke English, or even German or French. By now, I was beginning to think I'd be sleeping in a park, if I could find one. Although it wasn't cold, I carried my camera and expensive lenses and wasn't keen on sleeping out in the city alone.

Finally, after block upon block, I heard one key keeper respond to me with those magic words, "*Si, si.*" Yes, the doorkeeper indicated in Spanish. He spoke softly; I could barely hear him. But it meant I would have a room to sleep in.

The woman in charge quickly descended several flights of stairs and greeted me at the door and led me to my room up those several flights. She had a kerchief of some sort on her head, and I assumed it was part of her sleeping attire. She was happy for the money but grumpy about getting up at this hour. Fine enough! She did her job quickly, collected the rate from me, showed me the common kitchen I could use, and disappeared.

Next morning, I got up late. After packing up, I peeked into the small kitchen that morning where a young woman—I assumed a Spaniard as she spoke Spanish and no English—with a big smile was cooking her breakfast. The kitchen had a small table with an ordinary tablecloth, blue and white squares, and a window at the end by a small refrigerator next to a small sink. I saw wallpaper, but the pattern and colors are vague now in my memory. The Spanish girl turned to me, to her right from the stove, with a smile so huge it stood out like Mt. Rushmore. She insisted I eat part of her breakfast. We couldn't talk but tried sign language and a few words. I showed her on a little map that I was from America. Something felt interestingly strange. She was almost overly friendly and was very enthusiastic to see me. No, nothing of romance about it, just someone giving me a hand. I couldn't put my finger on it—but even then, that morning, before the rest of the day unfolded, I had the clear feeling that it was as if she'd expected me. I can't say why I felt this. It was the kind of intuitive feeling I would say to myself, "No, it can't be." But I hadn't learned myself well enough yet, and I was still early on my path to spiritual awareness. She was quite determined I would have some breakfast, I remembered, and seemed to be on a mission to take care of me—a mission she didn't hide from me very well, or perhaps she didn't even try to. I couldn't shake her and this experience from my thoughts that morning as I caught a public bus and headed back into the city.

It was critical I be on that train that evening. We had no cell phones in those days, and without keeping our meeting place and time, Karen and I might miss each other. Later, I was kicking myself for not having a backup plan with Karen in case something went wrong.

Three hours after leaving breakfast and parting from the young woman, I was down in Barcelona, exiting a museum, and stepped into the bright sunshine. It was lunchtime, around two in the afternoon, and people packed the sidewalk. I wandered across the street that bordered a park to get my bearings, and I started down the sidewalk to the right down a small incline. Not knowing quite where I was going next, I was looking all around, trying to figure out where I was, and I ran straight into someone walking towards me in that crowd. And who was it but … the very girl from my hotel, and I didn't even know her name. Go figure. Out of almost two million people in that city, the only one I know I run into? How many sidewalks? And I had just crossed the street and turned to the right? Coincidence? I looked twice, not believing my eyes. I thought my eyes were playing tricks. Beyond that, she still held that immensely huge, bright smile, revealing her nice white teeth. We smiled a clumsy greeting and stepped aside to avoid a head-on body collision, and both of us took another step before realizing the strangeness of the situation and turned around to stop and greet each other again. I stopped and turned around. She did the same. We were very surprised—at least I was—but we could not say an intelligible word with our language barrier.

It wasn't a long encounter, but it gave me a lot more to think about that day than the sites of Barcelona. How strange that was to meet her again. But coincidences do happen …

Towards evening, I followed my map and found the train depot to take the high-speed train to Paris and meet Karen. What I soon found out, however, was that there were three train stations in Barcelona, and this was not the one I needed in order to meet Karen. Time was flying, and yet I couldn't figure out which depot was *my* depot. I waited in a long line to ask the clerk, who did not speak English, and who then tried to brush me aside. I didn't speak Spanish, tough luck. By now, however, I was firm and determined to get an answer. Finally, he touched his finger on the map to indicate another train depot. I raced outside and boarded a bus to take me in that direction.

But when I got to the station, it was another also-ran. Two down and one to go. But how would I get there? Time was rushing faster now. Toting some snacks for the train and my suitcase, I hurried out to the sidewalk to look for another bus.

It was nearly dark by now. The streetlamps were beginning to flicker on. I found the bus stop I thought I needed. It was getting later, and I was beyond worried. But all I could do was wait for the bus, so I stepped up to the spot under the sign where it would stop and did what I am worst at—wait.

The next few moments are totally clear in my memory, even to this day.

A blue bus rambled up the street after a few minutes and stopped at the light a short distance away before reaching me. When the light changed, it pulled up in front of me. I picked up my suitcase and little bag of snacks and went to step in the bus's rear door, which properly opened.

I waited for a passenger coming down the little step to disembark, and who stepped out of the bus to greet me but … the same girl I'd twice encountered that day. Her smile was huge and lit up the area. I was dumbfounded and frozen in place.

What in the world …? How could this be, I thought. What is going on? Hundreds and hundreds of streets and buses, and now the one and only person who seemed to befriend me in Barcelona. Again!

Cars whizzed by. Pedestrians walked past, although the sidewalk wasn't too crowded. All of this I noticed on some subconscious level, but my attention was on her. I looked her in the eye. She seemed a bit shy and didn't want to stare. I really needed help. Could she …?

I didn't step into the bus. It left without me. I stood on the sidewalk with her facing me, trying to know what to say, and began rambling in English. I still didn't even know her name. She didn't know a word of what I was saying; but no matter, we stuck together.

She stood there, with the big, beautiful smile I had seen first at the little breakfast kitchen miles away. What was she doing here? Standing right in front of me? Looking right up at me, as if she had nothing else to do?

How could I have run into her a third time? How was this even possible? Questions kept flying in my face. I had never heard the word synchronicity then, few had.

Blown away by the strangeness of the situation, and already frazzled because of being lost and late, I was humbled, stunned, and weakened. I like control as much as the next person, and like any other guy, I don't like asking for help. I suppose some people would have brushed this off and kept moving—and gotten on that bus. But I had to listen to my heart; it said, "Stop."

For us to meet again and at that exact moment in time and at that exact place ... I realized I was at the mercy of someone or something, and my life was not in my own control. So I relaxed to get my bearings.

She looked happy. She always did. Did she ever stop smiling? I was simply stunned, and I broke into a huge smile also. We couldn't speak, but something said she wasn't surprised to see me at all. I wondered if she had been guided somehow, in some way, to help me that day. My relinquishing control and relaxing let different—odd— thoughts enter my mind. I wasn't one to think about angels in the flesh helping us out, but ... my meeting this girl ... again. What else could I think? It crossed my mind within a few minutes.

Gathering ourselves, we sat down at a table at a little sidewalk café by the bus stop. I wanted to buy her anything I could, but she refused. I did order a beverage for her, but I didn't see her drink it. I asked her name, but it was a foreign name to me and quite difficult for me to pronounce, once she figured out what I was asking. She spoke it fast and quite softly, almost mumbled her name when I asked. I leaned over and put my ear up to her mouth and even asked twice, but never got satisfaction. I got out a pen and she wrote it on an envelope, but I could never read it. I showed her on the map where I thought I was going—where I believed the correct train station to be. She understood. I pointed to my camera to indicate I'd like to take her picture, and she nodded that it was okay. But the picture came out blurry when I developed my film back in the United States.

When we stood up, she gently led me across town, changing from bus to bus, until we eventually arrived at the station with the train to Paris. She led me through the depot and into the train area, even to my train car where I had reservations. We were on time, but barely. It wasn't but a few minutes when the train began to move. Then, standing outside, she watched and waited until the train pulled out, which is when I saw her for the last time. We parted with a gentle and mysterious wave. Her big, bright smile had now faded into a look of satisfaction with a calmness about it.

Nothing in the visible, conscious world can explain something like this. Nothing. It lies outside normal experience. It defies scientific reasoning. It goes beyond coincidence. Yet, in retrospect I realized, this amazing incident fit into the trip and my life perfectly. As with meeting the German couple wanting to go to Masada, I was always bumping into the right people or seeing the right poster or having the right things happen to me—each at precisely the perfect time—and leading me in a direction that spurred on my development towards spiritual consciousness. It was the spiritual life I sought in truth, the life in my prayers. Given how much I read, I could easily have been a pure academic in my life—a theological or philosophical scientist, like western religion is built on, a "just give me the facts" kind of guy. But this experience and others later made me realize that, to be honest, there is a spiritual world close by all the time. Filled with angels or spiritual guides or the Holy Spirit or whatever name we give, it matters not, this dimension waits for us to access it and benefit from it.

I didn't have fully formed ideas about those happenstances at the time. For the most part, I thought I had good luck. But with the girl with the big smile, I knew that I'd had an extraordinary experience that hard, cold facts could not adequately explain. This incident stuck in my mind over the next leg of my unconventional journey to finding spiritual awareness, and it planted the seed in my thinking that there could be someone or "someones" guiding me from another dimension of reality. My belief system was not closed, but it wasn't geared for something so out of the ordinary as this. It seems it had to be opened gradually. Science clearly ruled in these days. Even mainstream religion looked for hard facts and denied the possibility of miracles. And although my running into this girl—twice—was a fact, the reasons behind it fell outside of science and seemed to float through the air like a spiritual kind of meeting.

Even without putting words to that experience, it opened me up to be guided in my life more and more by these kinds of "coincidences," believing they came from a source greater than visible, hard, cold facts. They would serve me well in my mission to come into full spiritual awareness, and if I denied them, I would be denying part of the very thing I was looking for.

Later, I realized I was being led graciously and slowly on my spiritual path so that I could experience the questioning—and remember that—in order to develop compassion for others. As I had resisted, I could understand how others could resist spiritual conceptions and remain unwilling to reach their own place of spiritual consciousness.

For the moment, still reveling in my "good luck," I was thrilled finally to be on the high-speed train to Paris. And I did arrive in time to meet Karen. We each had a room in a hotel on the Left Bank and roamed the Louvre, Notre Dame, the Eiffel Tower, Versailles, and other tourist sites over the next days.

We enjoyed French cuisine immensely so eating at French restaurants with Karen was a double delight. Because I knew more French than she, I had a wonderful time impressing her and hearing her laugh when I spoke to waiters and different people we met. I especially remember the small around-the-corner place that had a beautiful wooden bar and only three tables and a French poodle that wore dark glasses and a hat and sat up to the bar and entertained us while we delighted in the food. Perhaps I am an artist at heart. I just like to see delectable cuisine prepared with gusto and presented as an artistic creation. Supposedly, this indicates my romantic side, but I truly believe you'll find no food better than that in France.

Karen kept me laughing. How different from our many pensive visits eight months earlier back in the States. She was wonderfully knowledgeable about what to see in Paris and made the city more enjoyable for me. Without her, I would never have noticed or appreciated so much in the Louvre. I would never have bothered to visit beautiful Versailles. And I would never have had such good company. But she, too, benefited from the trip. I saw the side to Karen I had known back in college. I knew she was on her way to recovery and would do well.

After a few days, however, it was time for us to go our separate ways: me to Scandinavia and Karen to other parts of France. We didn't talk much anymore about our spouses. Time was creating space for grief to find a settled and comfortable place in our souls. I saw Karen back home only once or twice more after the summer. Some relationships are meant to serve us for a certain period of time, which this one did big time for me, and then it is time to move forward and away. Still, knowing Karen and having had her wonderful care for me during that time is a cherished memory.

On the flight home from Europe at the end of the summer, I reflected on what had happened that summer. My suitcase was packed with rolls of film to develop, and my heart looked forward to getting back home, but I wondered where home was.

The *why* question was no longer on my mind. Instead, I was now looking ahead to what I would do. I had learned that to do something good for others would be a big part of my healing. But what? I had been faced with the horrifying fact of the Holocaust and its systematic and cold-hearted murder of people simply for what they were, their nationality and religious beliefs. I sensed that the world held far more people who were suffering some sort of betrayal or injustice than I had imagined, and I felt a small measure of their pain in my heart, no longer just shelving such thoughts into a convenient, out-of-the-way bookcase in my mind. Altogether, these experiences were shaping me to feel more compassion for myself—for my own mistakes and my flailing efforts to put grief behind—as well as for the feelings of others.

And that empathy, in turn, was leading me further onto my spiritual path, creating a concrete foundation to my purpose, and developing greater spiritual awareness.

CHAPTER 6

I also remember the moment my life changed, the moment I finally said, "I've had it! I know I'm much more than I'm demonstrating mentally, emotionally, and physically in my life." I made a decision in that moment, which was to alter my life forever. I decided to change virtually every aspect of my life. I decided I would never again settle for less than I can be.

Anthony Robbins
Motivational Teacher

Landing in Seattle, I looked forward to an enthusiastic greeting from my dog, Smokey, at my parents' home. He'd been my good friend for fourteen years, much of them my formative years. Who else loves us unconditionally as our good dogs do? My English/Welsh grandfather, Thomas, had given him to me after my childhood dog, Squirt, was run over by a car. This was the grandfather whose hair I thought was shaded like the color of my beard, full grown by now. I was eager to see Smokey's smiling eyes as he jumped up to me and held out his paws.

But when I got home, no Smokey greeted me.

"Where's Smokey?" I asked and had an empty feeling at the same time.

"Well …," my dad said from the front porch, and he told me the story. "I didn't want you to know while you were away," he began.

Smokey was gone. His arthritis had gotten the best of him. He had become so crippled with arthritic pain that the best thing to do was to put him down. Smokey knew it was his time, my dad said. The ordinary, medium-sized mixture of a dog, a kind of smoky coloring of brown, black, and even red covering his coat, had gotten to where he could barely drag his rear feet behind him. But when my dad lifted him into the front seat to go to the vet, he leaped up and landed on all fours in the back seat, instead, with a special spurt of energy to try to get away. He knew. He knew this was the end for him, and he wasn't eager to go. I like to think he was hoping I'd get home and say goodbye before he was sent to his happy hunting ground.

Dad said, "I'll never have another dog."

My parents had looked after Smokey while I was in college and then, again, while I was in Europe, so Dad obviously felt deeply attached to Smokey, as I did. He had strong sentimental feelings, and for Welshmen such as my dad, tears flow easily. Putting a dearly loved pet down hurts, but it was best for Smokey.

To tell you the truth, when I found out I'd lost Smokey, it was very hard to remember to practice the lesson I had learned about giving thanks for what I had had, rather than only to feel badly about what I'd lost. I had to keep relearning the gratitude lesson with each new grief experience.

So now what?

In the world scene, this was a time of political shake-up. The country had turned against the Viet Nam war. Both a president and his brother Robert Kennedy had been murdered, along with Martin Luther King Jr. Riots in streets were destroying cities. Under pressure, President Johnson was not running for re-election. Woodstock was about to gather the heart of youth looking for respite from so much turmoil. In my northwestern corner of the country, we heard about people moving north from California to form communes in the rural Oregon wilderness. None of these groups seemed to be highly organized. Rather, they were places where people of like minds gathered. Young people with money, sometimes with their parents' money, bought a farm in an outlying area and invited their friends to come live with them. Although fairly new to the culture, drugs frequently flowed among commune members, and that contributed to the gathering of youths to such groups in Oregon.

More than anything, the growth of these communes demonstrated that our country was lost in a cultural war. Coming back from my European journey, I felt as if I had a new world to adjust to. History was spinning like a top and turning sharply. The early Baby Boomers, born in the late 1940s, now heading into their twenties, were clashing head-on with their parents' values. University presidents were losing control, war was being fought in streets, public figures were being assassinated. A whole generation was saying, "Enough is enough." The concept of a counterculture took on life, spread throughout the country, and developed strong roots, especially on the West Coast.

The unrest on the larger scale mirrored my own personal experience of an unsettled future. I had no idea what to do.

Word came that the headquarters of the ministry campus organization I had been involved in was starting a school for those who wanted to support the work as scholars, and they said I could come there. That seemed to make sense for me at that time.

After a few days at my parents' place, I packed up my Rover 2000TC (a popular English sports sedan at the time), the car I had bought in the spring to replace Nancy's and my VW sedan, and headed south to California, to headquarters.

On my way through Oregon, I pulled off at the head of the Willamette Valley in Eugene to see some friends. But I found I had more friends there than I realized. Several had recently moved to the area, and they, too, were looking for a deeper spiritual experience. Just as the nation was going through cultural turmoil, so the religious world was transitioning into new ways of doing religion, and these friends were young people who had left the same campus ministry that I had and had moved to Eugene from around the nation. One heard about what was happening there and then another and another until Eugene had become a gathering place for those on a spiritual trek for truth and reality. They were a part of the mix in the country's upheaval, a religious counterculture, and the group and what it was searching for fit perfectly into what I wanted.

Seek and you shall find, is an old saying in the Sermon on the Mount. Or as wise, tough, and crusty old prophet Jeremiah said, "You will seek me and find me, when you search for me with all your heart." What I had found in my life so far in terms of religion wasn't even in the ballpark of what my heart longed for in spirituality. But I was seeking.

When I stopped in Eugene, I discovered about fifty or so former members of my college ministry organization, Campus Crusaders for Christ, who had felt betrayed, hurt, and disillusioned by their crusade experience. Like me, they were looking for a spiritual experience that gave more than what we had encountered on campus and hoped to create it there. They happily welcomed me, which made me feel good and gave me reason to rest in Eugene for a while.

If I had to pick a place to land, Eugene was ideal, and the Crusade organization expecting me in California was glad I stayed. As it turned out, the school didn't start at that time anyway. So I became an assistant to the regional director, based in Eugene.

Home of the University of Oregon, Eugene was also quickly becoming one of the centers of counterculture activity, the new consciousness activity, along with places like Berkeley, UCLA, Santa Barbara, and other universities across the country. Oregon itself, among the most freedom-thinking states of the West, was a rich seedbed for independent thinking, continuing a tradition started more than a hundred years before.

In the nineteenth century, pioneers had traveled the old Oregon Trail, winding across America to valleys of the Pacific Northwest. They had left everything behind, fording rivers, crossing prairies, and hoisting themselves over mountains to seek the fulfillment of their hopes and dreams—a chance to start new lives. Now, a century later, when I stopped, the valley again became a budding place of new life, filled with the aspirations of a new generation. Young people were streaming in from all over, propelled by a dream of forming a new world of a simpler, communal life. I was searching for a way to build on my dream of a deeper experience with God, and just as landing in Oregon had made sense to pioneers decades before, it made sense for me and my colleagues from around the country then.

I think of us Campus Crusade throw-offs as pioneers, too, roughing it along a spiritual trail, looking for new meaning in life. We never became a commune; although we were generous with each other, and we all felt genuine love permeated the sharing. It felt good to be even a part of this movement.

The Campus Crusade advocated the idea that bigger is better. But we had seen the glaring weaknesses of its "Win the World in Our Generation" philosophy and wanted to try different ideas in this offshoot in Eugene. Now we wanted small meetings—what we called church—in living rooms. We looked for substance and depth, quality before quantity.

Denominational churches felt dead to us. They were more concerned with holding onto past teachings and practices or involvement in secular politics. Many of us had come from a traditional church background of one sort or another. Independent Bible churches felt too confining and about the same as denominational churches to us. Probably the movement closest to ours was the Charismatic Movement, but we were not Pentecostals.

When gathered, maybe twenty-five or thirty of us, we usually stood in a circle and sang meaningful songs, many from the Gaithers—Bill Gaither wrote rich, spiritual songs during this period—and others shared with the Charismatic Movement. We didn't need accompaniment. One person would think of a song and get us started, and then another would follow. This could go on for two hours. Sometimes, we felt so good we would find ourselves arm in arm, swaying back and forth to the tunes.

Other times, one of us would share a Bible verse and say a few words. But even though Campus Crusade taught summer studies to get staff theologically educated, in the field, we were trained to use only about eight verses, and most of the people there knew only those few. In other words, Campus Crusade did not give us much to build on for depth. We had enthusiasm and desire, but we lacked substance, teaching, and direction. Unfortunately, we didn't know how naïve and vulnerable we actually were.

The arts and music arenas gave no better guidance and, instead, merely reflected our lack of grounding. Sometimes I found myself humming a couple of popular songs, such as Kris Kristofferson's "Me and Bobby McGee," an existentialist story of two wandering nomads, getting all they could today because tomorrow may never come. I felt like a wandering nomad myself.

Frank Sinatra sang "My Way," telling us to follow our own path. As wonderful as that sounded, being true to ourselves, we still didn't know what "my way" was for any of us. But we pursued it as best we could.

Two English young men, Andrew Lloyd Webber and Tim Rice, shocked the world with the hit musical, *Jesus Christ Superstar*, which portrays a new view of Jesus and a new theology that fit with the times. It threw out the old thinking about Jesus as only God and challenged us to consider other possibilities of him as man as well.

As I glance back at my experience in Eugene within the context of the upheaval in the world at the time, I realize we weren't crazy. Our attempt to shed the old ways of faith and religion and find a new way of spirituality was simply in the spirit of the time. We were traveling the same path everyone else was, searching for answers, looking for greater meaning in our lives, wanting not only to discard what no longer worked but also to replace it with something better.

With all the turmoil of the country's up-ended standards surrounding us, we also felt a tremendous positive energy. We could bring about a positive change in the world, or at least our small part of it, and this was the time to do so. And so in Eugene, I felt I was on the cutting edge of life in the world.

But I also did something else there that I would never have expected, something that not only helped me in my personal grief but also gave me a chance get going on the "what" I had decided to do when I quit asking why.

CHAPTER 7

*Writing is a form of therapy; sometimes I wonder
how all those who do not write, compose or paint can
manage to escape the madness, the melancholia, the
panic fear which is inherent in a human situation.*

Graham Greene
Writer

After the previous winter's heart-warming visits with my friend
Karen, my marvelous summer in Europe and Israel, and now
anticipation of fresh spirituality in our budding house church
in Eugene, I might have felt only the promise of the future. Instead,
mixed emotions ran through me as the anniversary of the wreck
approached and a wave of renewed grief threatened to overwhelm
me. I continued to give thanks for what I had had, and I was looking
ahead, no longer stuck in the past and asking why it had happened.
But still, a black hole lurked in the shadows.

I had made progress. The summer had taught me the value
of letting the unanswerable question of why this had happened fly
away. In my wounds, I had identified with the victims of Masada and
Dachau. But learning the big-time lesson of giving gratitude back for
what I did have had helped immensely in keeping me from sitting
around and feeling sorry for myself. Sometimes I found complaining
was easier than living in thanks, however, and a gratitude attitude
was something I needed to remind myself of many times because it
was easy to slip.

I had been in Eugene about six weeks and, with help from
friends, had found a cute, little, temporary room to rent. Mentally, I
was settling in for what I thought could be an extended visit to the

pioneer country of Oregon during the countercultural revolution. How long would I be there? Would I build a life there, or would this be a temporary stop on life's journey for me? I didn't know. I didn't know if I was in the early or end stages of grief recovery. How would I know until I went through it? I was just living day to day and happy to have good friends around with similar spiritual aspirations. But sad feelings erupted almost every day.

So, now in my rented room on the outskirts of Eugene on October 18, after about two weeks of unloading my car and moving in, I was lying in bed at about eleven o'clock at night. Moving shadows from the lights of a passing car occasionally played on the off-white walls and ceiling of the small room. Eyes half-open and half-asleep, I drifted along in the alpha state. I remember this so clearly I can put myself back into that bed and that moment as if it is happening to me again, right now. Once more a car's light scanned shadows across the ceiling, and then I had the strangest experience.

Suddenly, in my mind's eye, I began to see a parade of episodes of a book running through my imagination, parts of Nancy's and my story, all in color and with even a name for it. The epiphany-like experience came unanticipated, out of the blue. I could already feel this creative, unexpected process releasing healing endorphins throughout my body and my mind—my heart, too, I'm sure.

I need to emphasize that I saw things, images in my head. It was like a short video, running snippets across my mind, from left to right. I saw parts of my relationship with Nancy, stories to tell. I saw our love. I saw the crash and felt a twinge of pain shoot through my stomach. I even saw parts of the process of my healing.

I was so excited I needed to stop and analyze what I had actually experienced in a calm, down-to-earth manner. What I saw was a book about our story. I would write it. It would include the romance Nancy and I had experienced, the accident, and the lessons I had learned about grief and sorrow from a faith basis. The purpose was to share what I had found in terms of faith in a time of grief and tragedy for others to learn from.

I pondered a few minutes over the title that had come to me, *At Least We Were Married*. Nancy's dream had taken its first step; my dream of a beautiful bride had come true in Nancy. Isn't it amazing I didn't have to labor over naming the book? I saw how the chapters would break down. I saw how the book would start. I jumped up, turned on the light over my little desk, got out paper and pen, and quickly wrote the first chapter. The words flowed like melted butter on a warm day, the chapter seemingly writing itself. The story in that first chapter had simply poured out of me and later published almost exactly as I had written it that night—to me it was holy. Tears slipped up into the corners of my eyes and ran onto the paper the whole time my pen was moving. On another piece of paper, I began scribbling out chapter titles and an outline. About two in the morning, I returned to bed but didn't fall asleep for several hours.

I think both my powerful revelation on the gurney in the hospital hallway and my serendipitous experience with the young woman in Barcelona had prepared me to receive a spiritual experience like this—and certainly, it was spiritual. The only way I can explain the gurney experience of feeling utter joy while my body lay in contorted pain and the Barcelona experience of meeting the woman "accidentally" three times in one day and a vision-like experience of writing this book when it turned out so well is spiritually.

Was this book, though, the mission, the life's purpose, I'd been searching for? Was this the *what* I'd decided I needed to find? Turned out the answer was no, but this project fed into it in a large way. At the time, I didn't realize that the one most helped by the book would be me, simply by writing it out. I stumbled into this method of helping myself to heal—how writing my story did as much for me as for any reader. In those days no one said that helping someone else boomerangs back around to help you, too. I only knew I had a *what* ahead of me now that I was no longer plagued by the question of *why*.

It would have been easy for me to sink totally into myself during those lonely, rudderless days, even more than I already had. Everyone I knew felt sorry for me, which only made it easier to feel sorry for myself. Some people wondered why I didn't descend even deeper into this unhealthy state, which, of course, was further motivation to make sure it didn't happen. To fall into a lost pool of living death would have been failure to me. Like the aftershocks of an earthquake, I still carried a massive load of latent, emotional pain that constantly fought for control of my streaming background thoughts. I was even more frustrated because I knew I had a purpose in my new life, but I didn't know what it was.

Fortunately, I believe in compassion, and perhaps this is what helped me shift my mental gears at the time and to understand and have compassion for myself with the wounded soul. At the time, it was not easy to quit thinking about myself, so I worked toward a sympathetic understanding of myself—of why I was focusing too much on myself. I needed to understand myself without pity, to accept what I felt—a grief most natural in my circumstances—without sinking into a pit of despair, to let the pain flow through without holding me up in any way.

So this was another reason this book project appealed to me; I knew I would think about something besides myself as I wrote it. Yes, it sounds strange, doesn't it? After all, it was a book about me and my experiences, so I would naturally focus on myself and my life, but I also knew I would write it to help other people. I was beginning to turn outward and be aware of others and what they needed, not just me and my needs.

I knew instantly that after the excitement of that night, when I lay back in bed, that my work was cut out for me, and it would be for the next nine months, as it turned out.

Now I had a mission. Discipline took over. I planned a daily routine. Ran three miles a day. Bought notebook paper and a couple of new pens. And I kept it to myself. I had a job, and I had friends to meet with, but I decided I would not tell anyone what I was doing, just utilize every spare moment and quietly continue writing. As Regional Assistant, I went out of town a lot with Crusade staff on assignments, but I had quite a bit of free time when we were home. So I used it to complete the story, doing it "my way," as Frank Sinatra had been singing. I went to work.

Statistics stood against my getting published. In the Eugene library, I found that one book in seven that was submitted actually got published at that time (today it's less than one in one hundred). Odds were even worse that it would be purchased and read. Only a small percent of books that finally were published at that time broke even for the publisher. Then, as now, publishers depended on a few big sellers to carry the rest, and I planned mine to be one of those that carried others. I knew I would have to do my all-out best, and yet I was inexperienced. To compensate, I decided to leave no detail uncovered and to read up as best I could on how to write a book.

After the way the book came to me that night with such clarity, I had confidence. It was a feeling of certainty, just like the feeling I had lying on the gurney in the hallway in the hospital—I was certain I would live then, and I definitely believed I had a purpose for living; something I was meant to do with my life. It was a wonderful feeling, this sense that no matter what happened in the little details, no matter what anyone said, I knew I was heading in the right direction. I knew my mission, I had a sense of my greater purpose, and I knew I would receive help along the way—just as in Barcelona. Maybe it was faith. Maybe it was God—that's what I believe. But I did know along the way that whatever I was doing at the time was fitting into a larger life picture for me, with a purpose that I might only later understand.

I *knew* from somewhere inside me at that time that this book was destined to be read by thousands, if not even more. That sounded arrogant even to me, but how else could I honestly accept a belief like that? I was trying hard to be humble about it because I knew I would have to work hard, concentrate, and listen to the ring and rhythm of each sentence many times to get it just right.

As you can imagine, I was both surprised and not surprised when the book was published about two years later and, according to my count, sold more than half a million copies, which was quite a high number back then. It was also translated into Spanish and Dutch. There I was, alone at a desk with pen and paper, but out there were masses who would read what I had written and benefit from the telling.

An interesting and unanticipated benefit came about as I wrote—
the karma rule. I didn't know the word karma back then, but the idea
is that the more we give, the more we receive. I thought I was giving
help to others, but in greater measure, I was receiving that for myself.
As I wrote the story, I relived it all: the courtship, the wedding, the
accident, the lost honeymoon. I felt the pain and sorrow over again.
But each time I relived those emotions in writing, some of them were
released, as they needed to be released. Some days, memories came
up that I did not know were there. I saw some events at the wreck
scene in my memory for the first time, and it was as if I was in the
wreck all over again.

Some people told me not to think of these things, but I found
that if I relived them and raised them to the surface, they could be
washed clean of the polluting pain. The load could be lightened. The
tears I was too preoccupied to shed the first time around now flowed
a lavishing cleanse, sometimes daily. As they came out as I wrote *At
Least We Were Married*, they helped me to release my feelings and
move my emotional and spiritual healing forward faster.

Many people have done exactly what I did during my process:
They have wept—sometimes for sorrow and yet, many times, to
overcome intense grief.

As the great psychiatrist and Viennese Holocaust survivor
Viktor Frankl observed: "Emotion, which is suffering, ceases to be
suffering as soon as we form a clear and precise picture of it." My
writing out the story was getting out the fine details of the story and
the feelings I had for it, and that turned the emotion away from suffering and into acceptance. Putting my story down on paper helped
in two ways—in my writing it and in my reading it, strange as this
may seem. The writing let my emotions flow out, and the reading
allowed me to step outside the story and experience it as a third party
would, with objectivity.

I want to make a critical point I have learned over time through
the horror of this grief. We all have much grief in our lives. Either
little things build up or unexpected big things arise, and they all
smack us down. The better we deal with the grief, the better people

we become and less of a drain on others and society. If we work at it, we may even recover and excel to the point of contributing massive good back into the world, something we never would have done if the loss hadn't happened. By releasing the grief—working through the process to be able to do this—we can actually have a fuller life than we'd ever believed possible.

But sharing my grief, being willing to open up about it—that was an answer to eventual healing and even achieving a fuller life, and I found this to be true for me and for many other people. It is critical to release our inner suffering and grief. To hide it is impossible because it pops up from the backside and catches us unaware. To cover it up and stuff it away only creates festering. I found we must feel the pain until it feels less painful. Sometimes it is so severe we clearly need a professional coach to help hold us together. If possible, if we have someone who loves us unconditionally, it helps to share what we feel until those overwhelming emotions have been washed and, thus, lessened.

I have seen the effects of ignoring the grief, and the pain never really goes away. I saw this firsthand with a good farmer I once knew whose wife died of cancer, leaving him with four sons. Soon after she passed, he sold the farm, bought a large truck, and began hauling grain to a port up on the Great Lakes. The trucker businessman, unfortunately, stopped up his grief; not only did he not talk about his wife's death with anyone, but he also hid all his emotions surrounding her death. Later, he moved into my area, and only much later did I learn of the burden he was carrying inside his soul.

Eventually, he remarried. I visited him and his new wife in his small home near a lake. He was kind, cheerful, and humble, but something did not feel quite right to me, as if there was something to be said that was left silent. Soon a strike in the grain-moving process went on to shut his business down. So he had lost his wife, he had given up his farm, and now his business was shut down. Those things added up to three major griefs—enough to put any man or woman in a sad place of suffering. Throw in the stiff upper lip of his Nordic-heritage personality, and the dilemma was devastatingly compounded.

Not surprisingly, I later found out, he never spoke of his first wife after she died. Never, ever, the sons told me, would he allow them to mention their dead mother. Not even a whisper. If they started, he'd shut them right up quickly and firmly, they said.

In other words, he bottled up his feelings and didn't want to talk about them or hear about them or anyone else's. No one saw any tears. Nor did he have any discussion with his family, pastor, or friends. He simply tried to go on with life and ignore the grief piling up inside him. I've always believed that if he ever started to release the sorrow, he must have felt an unfamiliar pain he didn't want, so he shut it down as best he could.

But it was there still in him, and he could not contain it forever. Eventually, all the memories and sorrows locked up inside him burst out, like a violent volcanic eruption. One day, he dropped his wife off at a Bible study, returned home, stepped out back into his woods with a 22 rifle, sat on a log, and ended his life with a bullet between his eyes.

This man's response to grief was the opposite of what I experienced when I wrote my book. As I put each thought, sentence, paragraph, and page together, the bottle of sorrow and grief was open and pouring out freely, but it never got the best of me. I even had days of happiness—joy and gratitude that I could write and work through the process. But at the same time, I felt sadness over such a horrifying tragedy happening to anyone. The dam burst frequently, and out flowed beautiful, salty tears.

I believe that, at the time of the accident, I was so preoccupied with other things that some of the sorrow had never risen to the surface and been released as it was during this time of writing. I think many experience this delayed reaction. When a traumatic event hits us, we cope as best we can. We can handle only so much, face only so much grief, and some of the sorrow remains buried. So sometime later, unexplored sadness or grief creeps up on us, and we might wonder why—hadn't we dealt with that already? But it comes when we can deal with it; so at that point, we need to face it. We're better for having gone through the emotional release.

Giving ourselves permission to grieve runs counter to what some say we should do. "Be strong," people say. "Put it behind you, and get on with your life." Men, especially, have a hard time opening up—and believing it's okay. Our society seems to encourage this bottling up. For instance, I once heard a leading radio talk show host condemn George Bush Sr. for shedding some tears while giving a speech after he retired. Former President Bush, by this time, was probably in his eighties. How disgraceful of this talk show personage to condemn a man for crying. I have seen Little League coaches berate young boys for crying, which is even more disgraceful. Men can cry, or it wouldn't be in their genetic or physiological make-up. Often, men who allow the tears to flow will become healthier and stronger once they do.

As I wrote *At Least We Were* Married, the book became my friend. It had a meaningful place in my life, and it was part of me. And, although I would publish the story and share it with hundreds of thousands, I wrote it first and foremost for me. Like an eternal gravestone, it marked my feelings at that time in my life.

The diary of the Jewish teenager Anne Frank, written while she hid in an attic during World War II to escape the Nazis, illustrates this same idea of the power of writing from the heart primarily for oneself. She was squeezed into that attic with not only her family but also strangers. She wrote her intimate feelings with captivating eloquence to her only friend, her diary. She revealed her blossoming transformation from child to young woman. Puberty is never easy, but her extraordinary circumstances made it even more challenging, and her diary shows how writing can be a tool for coping with distress.

When I was in Europe earlier that summer, I had climbed the steps in the house in Amsterdam, in the Netherlands, to wander through the hidden apartment of Anne Frank's family. Upon descending, I stepped into the little shop on the ground floor and purchased a paperback copy of her diary, which I had never read. I tucked it into my suitcase and grew to look forward to the end of each day's journey when I could read more of her story.

Anne did not write to publish; she wrote for her own purposes, as a catharsis, as a release of the pain she felt in her trying circumstance and to try to make sense of the craziness of her world. Everyone needs a friend, and when no one else is around or no one fully understands our pain, writing can fill that gap. Anne wrote as one friend to another—friend to herself and her diary. In my mind, I see her with a bright, rather innocent smile—obviously a teenager with hope in her eyes. Did I weep over the book? Did I laugh? Did I feel angry? You bet. All of these.

Anne wrote with simple clarity of what was happening around her as a means of coping with her world turned upside down. But she also wrote in a way that lets us understand what she experienced—we sit in her place and see and feel as she did. She is one of those remarkable people we call world changers, and her gift, unbeknownst to her, impacted me and continues to impact millions of people around the world. For many days during my trip, the story in her diary so captivated me that I found it more interesting than whatever else I was doing. It took my mind off myself, just as *At Least We Were Married* would take my readers' minds off their problems.

We all have a story, don't we?

I've learned that, while grief becomes a part of us and changes us permanently, it does not make us who we are. Instead, the way we deal with it shapes who we become. We get to decide how it will change us—into a bitter, angry, and depressed person or into a more open, loving, and happy person. In other words, our grief does not have to control us. By writing, feeling, and releasing that grief, we can take charge. And it's possible to do so for events that occurred as far back as early childhood and that we thought we had already dealt with.

Towards the end of writing *At Least We Were Married*, I discovered I needed to bring closure to the book and, in a sense, to that chapter of my life. I knew I needed to let go—or, at least, to take another huge step on the path to letting go—of the grief, and yes, of Nancy. I needed to do so if I was going to move into the next level of my new life. So, in the book's final chapter, I wrote an emotional goodbye message to Nancy. I sat down, inspired to write that chapter, but it was not just pages in a book to me. I was actually saying goodbye in my heart to Nancy. It was live. My heart felt the goodbye. Easy? No way. Very, very difficult. But I had to do it. I had to say goodbye to Nancy. Not that I would forget Nancy or what we'd shared. Not ever. Could never happen. But I could try to find the sunlight of a new day and a new life. She would want that, too, for me.

As I said goodbye to Nancy in that final chapter, I was also letting go of the book—my new best friend. Writing the story was something like constructing a granite monument I could plant in the world and leave behind as a marker. I could always return to the marker, as I would return to Nancy's gravesite, to revisit those emotions, events, and people in the book I knew so intimately.

Meanwhile, as I worked day by day in my rented room in Eugene on the banks of the McKenzie River to finish *At Least We Were Married*, I found a woman to type it. After that, I looked for a publisher. I had done it "my way"—I had written the book first and then looked for a publisher, which was opposite to normal procedure. But then, when was I ever "normal"?

I wasn't surprised when three publishers wanted the book. A former associate from the Campus Crusade era, Pete Gillquist, was working with the Christian-oriented Zondervan, and he convinced me it would do the best job of getting the book in front of the public, which it did.

When I turned the book over to Zondervan, I said goodbye to the story itself and never read it again—not until very recently. When it was published, many people wanted to give me an opportunity to forge a career from the book, but that did not feel right. I needed to leave the book as a gift for readers while I moved out and away from it.

Then it was over. Except for one thing. It became a best seller, which means I—and Nancy—touched thousands with messages of love and healing.

I've often wondered if Nancy's story, blended with mine in that book, did more than she ever could have accomplished, had she lived longer than she did in her short life. Nancy truly loved people. She loved people in a healthy way more than anyone I ever knew. Through the pages of that book, she has reached out with arms of love to readers. I'll never feel it makes up for what happened; that's not my point. It is simply a matter of taking something most horrible, placing it in the hands of God in my mind, going to work, and utilizing it for good.

Writing that book was my start on answering the *what* question I'd first asked on the sand dunes on the shores of the Red Sea the previous summer. I was ready to move beyond the philosophical *why* to the action-oriented *what*. During those first months in Eugene, I was able to walk through the story with more distance, more objectivity, and to shed more grief and wash away more sorrow. In giving, I received and did something that served the greater good.

CHAPTER 8

Now I know that there are three classes of people in the world. The first learn from their own experience—these are wise. The second learn from the experience of others—these are happy. The third learn neither from their own experience nor from the experience of others—these are fools.

Og Magdino
Writer

Now that *At Least We Were Married* was finished, I did my best to say goodbye, not only to Nancy but also to the book. Still residing in Eugene and soon moving from my rented room on the river into a house with some buddies, my next goals were to grow in my own spirituality and to support the desires our group of former Campus Crusaders trying to develop a house-type church.

I felt for my own well-being that I needed to move away from the book. But it left an emptiness. A major part of my life over the past two years—spent both writing and working with the publisher to get it printed—was gone. And, although I had said goodbye to Nancy in the last chapter and I did my best to follow through, realistically letting all that go took far more effort and time than my putting pen to paper. How could I? I was leaving behind not only the time devoted to work on the book; I was also parting with the four years of my life involving Nancy. In its place, I felt a huge hole. It felt as if I was back to square one, when I had first landed in Eugene. What next?

This time, I would get no blinding flash-in-the-night inspiration. In fact, I learned those experiences are rare.

Intuitively, I felt there was more to life than recognition or building up possessions or anything of life in material manifestation. French priest, theologian, and philosopher Pierre Teilhard de

Chardin captured the essence of our experiences on this planet as well as what I was beginning to feel at this period in my life: "We are spiritual beings having a human journey." At the time Teilhard de Chardin said that, it was an obscure thought for most of us. But over the decades, public consciousness has changed, and it is a philosophical-anthropological idea now known to multitudes, representing no one religion. It expresses how I was resonating to the spiritual aspect of life and how trying to live that was my primary endeavor.

Yet my advances in my spiritual quest could not have happened without my experiences over a ten-year span, beginning in college with the Campus Crusade for Christ, or CCC. The organization and its belief system slice into the heart of traditional evangelical religion in America, and at the time I participated—actively for more than three years and tangentially for another seven—they matched my religious background and beliefs and served as a foundation for the next period of my own spiritual life.

When Billy Graham was forming the Billy Graham Association in the 1940s, Bill Bright, originally from Oklahoma, came out of the same philosophy and, with Billy Graham's blessings, formed an evangelistic organization to convert college students to evangelical Christianity. Small at first, it began to grow over time to where now it has thousands of staff workers around the world. During my time on the staff, we were fewer and ranged from five hundred to one thousand, working only in America.

Initially, I had been attracted to Campus Crusade in college because I was planning to enter seminary right after graduation and Campus Crusade recruiters convinced me that Campus Crusade was God's A team. I could get into action right away, doing God's important work now. Whereas, going to seminary for four more years of professional theological and pastoral education and then serving as a pastor in a church was really going on to God's B team. In addition, Campus Crusade people looked sharp. They were effective speakers and leaders. And many drove snappy, cars. They knew exactly what they were doing—countering the impression of some college students that Christians were out of date and out of touch. The Crusaders did all they could to look contemporary, hip, effective, and appealing. They succeeded, and they had no trouble attracting college students to themselves and their meetings.

I liked the idea of starting into God's work immediately. And, really, why settle for second best? So when I joined, I leaped fully and passionately. No toe testing the waters for me, I dove in whole body and full force, like those dive-bombing ducks that hit the water from the fly and submerge. If I was to learn from mistakes I might make in early judgement, let them be big ones.

I was in Crusade, as we called it, as a career when I met Nancy and when we were married. I say career, but I think of Crusade as something more like a military campaign. It was more than a job to us—it became a twenty-four-hour-a-day way of life; and it was exciting. As in a war, we Crusaders had a united goal to win and win big. We aimed to covert the world to what we believed was the gospel in our generation.

And we wanted to do it our way. "My life should be unique," Ralph Waldo Emerson wrote as he set the pace for the American dream. The other members and I found that Crusade offered us a chance to be unique, special, out of the ordinary, and in a way that positively benefited the world. This going our own way also fit with the social-cultural revolution going on in America, especially on college campuses. Where our parents had obeyed authority without much questioning, members of my generation wanted to make personal decisions for ourselves. We rejected the idea of listening to authority figures, whether in the university, government, business, or church.

This cultural movement among the youth of America posed a few problems for those of us in Campus Crusade, given its style of management. Bill Bright was older than all the staff and had been successful in the early stages of Campus Crusade with an authoritarian style of leadership. He made the decisions. He set the rules. He assigned the staff. He oversaw everyone's work and dismissed non-performers. What had worked in the 1940s flew in the face of practices being embraced on campuses across the country in the 1960s. But the organization did not adapt.

One practice of Crusade that resulted from this dictatorial style, I found especially difficult to accept. Campus Crusade looked down upon anyone challenging it in any way, even in asking questions about its philosophy or practices. If a person dared ask a critical question, he or she risked falling into disfavor, particularly if the question revolved around core beliefs or values.

Once I experienced this defensive attitude from inside the organization, I so disliked it that I later avoided any religion that refused to allow questions from its followers. It created a closed and secretive system that was not open to the people and to the Spirit—and openness to one was the same as openness to the other. I found most religious organizations said they welcomed questions, but they really welcomed them only to a point—only as long as the question emerged from inside their own box of reality. But if their very reality was challenged, they closed the lid. Yet this response differed dramatically from what Jesus practiced. In the four Gospels, he answered every question, even those that challenged his reality. Little by little, as I understood this and how Jesus handled what others might call verbal attacks, I took Jesus, rather than any specific church, as my primary model.

Other members also found the style of management unacceptable. Eventually, all the regional leaders parted ways with Campus Crusade, and unfortunately, it was not done with grace and tact. Based upon comments around the country from departing staff members, I knew of no one who left over that eighteen-month period with understanding or compassion.

In leaving, these regional leaders were rejecting the authoritative leadership, but they were not throwing out the ideals of Campus Crusade. They looked to share in leadership but also take those ideals in a different direction. The regional leaders were focusing more on attaining a deeper spirituality through building a new house-type church ideal. I resonated to their new ideals to reach into God and a deeper, more satisfying sense of spirituality.

Bill Bright was caught as much by surprise at this change of attitude in the staff as were the nation's president over changes in the desires of the populace and university presidents coping with student sit-ins and radical campus activities. Bill Bright maintained his style of leadership as long as I was on staff, and although this turmoil certainly must have shaken him, he regrouped, immediately rebuilt his staff, and continued following his ideal.

A second area that began to bother me a lot during my second year was our operating as a sales organization for God. I had experience in direct sales and clearly saw the similarities. My first job out of high school was door-to-door selling of *Collier's Encyclopedias*. Most sets were around thirty volumes. In our sales training, we got a forty-five minute pitch to memorize—I still remember parts of it—once the customer opened the door. I used the lines, and I was sincere. I believed the books benefited a family, giving them access to knowledge and helping the children in their learning and school work.

Bill Bright had done something similar. We Campus Crusaders had a robotic type sales pitch, the four laws, as we called it, and a forty-five minute speech to give in fraternity houses and churches. To be successful, we did not need to think creatively—and actually, individual thinking could get in our way.

But I thought to myself, "Is this God's A Team? Are we truly doing God's ultimate work by using a short sales presentation over and over and over? Was there more to God and evangelism than that?" I began to think God is so big and his gospel is so precious, how can it be sold like an ordinary product?

I know people have been made right with God through the four laws and Campus Crusade work, but I also know that for many sincere converts, it didn't stick.

We were taught to keep moving, not let deadwood drag us down, keep finding new sales. What suffered was follow-up. We were to meet with the new convert the next day, and I did, as did most Crusaders. But over time, I found the promises we had made in the four laws were not working for the converts, promises like with Christ on the throne when they repeat the prayer, anxiety is replaced in their life by peace, frustration with purpose and power, and so on. But students were finding that they still had anxiety and frustration, especially at test time or when a girlfriend or boyfriend was breaking up with them.

Although I was having my doubts about the organization, and obviously, others were too, given how many left, I never realized the extent of the dissatisfaction until some years later. I ran into one of the female national leaders who had been on the staff itself for years but had departed, and she confided in me. She said, "Terry, it never worked for me. Inside, I always felt I was the same old person, but I tried. I couldn't tell this to anyone when I was on the staff. When the booklet on the Holy Spirit came out about spiritual breathing, that didn't work either."

A third concern centered on how we used a teaching called the Doctrine of Eternal Security. This doctrine says that once people said the prayer we taught them for salvation and were sincerely saved, they could never be lost, never lose their salvation. If they thought they had lost it, they were just mistaken. They were now "saved" and could not lose it whether we spent time nurturing them or not. So we Crusaders had them say the prayer, and then we moved on. Making the most converts in this form of evangelism mattered above all, and we had to keep moving and making new ones.

But gradually, this "convert and move on, regardless" went against my grain, especially when some of the teachers took a more extreme stance on pounding it home. However, my time with Campus Crusade for Christ allowed me to follow through on my goal in the organization—to lead people to Christ. And I successfully met the organization's goals, leading many into a prayer of conversion. I worked in all sincerity and took my part in these conversions as a privilege, which were quite thrilling for me, especially at first.

In addition, I learned some valuable lessons.

I realized I would take care not to yield my life to any man, any guru, or any spiritual leader. Instead, I would maintain my own integrity and give my inner connection only to the Spirit of God. If I was to find spiritual enlightenment, it would be just that—the Holy Spirit and me—not the Holy Spirit, a mediator, and then me.

I learned spiritual consciousness means a direct connection with God, and it means it is open to every one of us. Any religion that bases its connection with God only on a leader or a group of leaders who hear from God denies the rest of us our spiritual right. When we operate in an organization that expects us to follow like robots those human leaders, never think independently for ourselves, and follow church doctrine without questioning, we remain in the lower echelon of spirituality.

Crusade was good to me, supported me fully when Nancy was killed, and even after I left staff, supported me when my book came out. But I longed to move into the interior arena of the soul in my spirituality, and Crusade provided no guidance for that. Despite all the wonderful people I met in the organization, I found that even going with the flow of who is good and kind might not attain the goal of spiritual awareness.

Looking to replace what I had thought Campus Crusade would give me had made me feel right about staying in Eugene. Once more, I had people around me with similar spiritual goals, and many were friends from my Crusade days. For, without friends, where are we? I would feel at home—at least for the moment.

CHAPTER 9

Without friends, no one would want to live, even if
he had all other goods.

Aristotle

Aren't we destined to be happy? Each and every one of us? Consistently? Every day, no matter what? I don't mean Pollyanna denial-of-problems happiness, but realistic happiness.

This is what our group of former Crusaders in Eugene really wanted, and we believed the avenue to happiness was through a spirituality we could all share in together. We believed this was what in the first century was called church

Yet, two and a half years after Nancy's death, after I had left the Campus Crusade organization, and after I had published my book, I was marking time, emotionally and spiritually. At least I felt that way, even though later reflection showed deep, gradual internal movements were preparing me for the next phase of spiritual unfolding.

For work, I was building houses—which was fun for me. After finishing *At Least We Were Married*, my cousin and I had built a first house in Eugene on speculation and sold that one as I was getting into the home-building business—Thomas Homes, we called it. Building houses, developing land, and any other business-type venture were not my passions, but I did enjoy the work. And they allowed me time to pray and meditate in my own way and a practical daily life to test out results. The spiritual search and our group experience was, for me, my priority. I was happy to a degree, but even though I didn't know it, I was far from being emotionally recovered from the impact of the accident. I felt shy. I sometimes retired to be alone. I felt sorrow easily for other people's problems. I had had greater joy before Nancy's death, so I knew I was missing something. Looking back now, it was part of a deepening process.

Even though I was not totally happy, I had rejected the idea that we are here to be miserable and unhappy, cheerless and sad, smile-less, weighted down, heavyhearted, worried, fearful, humorless, downcast, discouraged, disheartened, in the dumps all the time, bored, moody, poverty-stricken, sick. Sticking to this conviction, I believe, allowed happiness finally to win out.

It was my conviction that to overcome the doldrums we have to make our happiness a top priority, our passionate purpose. As Jesus said, "Seek first the Kingdom of God, and everything else you want will be yours in addition."

But that great attitude seems to elude us. Later, I read countless books and virtually everyone in the world of self-improvement education agreed that a positive attitude works. But no one taught how to have that positive attitude. That is what I kept looking for—*how to do what my heart said I deserved*. I had the feeling of what I wanted, but I couldn't pin it down to something in actual practice. I had not seen any group that showed the genuine and authentic peace, love, and joy I was looking for. Because in Campus Crusade we were sent out to speak in churches, I had been on the inside operation of many, and I had not seen, felt, or witnessed it there, either.

So as I was seeking my own happiness, I was also working with the Eugene group of former Crusaders to form a church that was searching for the same—happiness for all its members. I didn't know exactly what this church would be, but I knew we'd recognize it when we found it. And we all believed it was a next step for each of us in finding our fulfillment and happiness in life through the Spirit.

Although we had entirely different educational backgrounds, ages, and careers, our group bonded around the common goal of seeking spiritual life. And no one was above anyone else. The spiritual aspect came above all and made it natural for us to come together.

After Campus Crusade had fallen apart, we all welcomed a way to fill the gap and begin to feel we were part of something bigger than any individual

Our goal of gathering together into a community of faith was good. But trying to be like the original church after Jesus died was not a good thing, as it turned out. Trying to operate like first century Christianity while living in the twentieth century had some major flaws. From somewhere, we had picked up the idea that the original church had sparkled like a diamond in pristine perfection. I went on to find out we were projecting our youthful idealism onto a wanting characterization. Perhaps we thought of the church as a kind of Garden of Eden that, just as Adam and Eve fell into sin, the church, over time, also fell into corruption and lost its perfection. We wanted to recover what was lost, and we thought that by getting back to the original, the one in Jerusalem we read about in the Bible following the death of Jesus, we would experience our group (church) happiness and perfection.

But as Bishop John Spong suggested in *Why Christianity Must Change or Die*, why not be a good religion that meets the world face to face, not confrontationally? We asked a similar question, and like Bishop Spong, we saw the need for change in religion so it would better meet the needs of people. "The Sabbath was made for man, not man for the Sabbath," the wise master of Galilee had taught. But unlike Bishop Spong, we thought the solution lay in what the original church had done. If trying to be pristine instead of contemporary left us vulnerable from the get-go, even in establishing the kind of church we wanted, so did our group's lack of education and experience in religion leave us open to being taken advantage of by charlatans.

Ours came in the form of Gene. At one time, Gene had been a talented Baptist Evangelist in Texas. Some unknown years earlier, he had become disenchanted with traditional church as he knew it and became attracted to the work of Witness Lee in Los Angeles, and a movement called the Local Church. Witness Lee had come across from China, where he was part of Watchman Nee's small-group, home-type churches, with the idea of duplicating their Chinese style of church in America. Watchman Nee was a famous Christian leader going back into the 1930s and, as he was about to be arrested by the Communists in China in 1962, sent Witness Lee to America to carry on their work here. Gene had sat under the teaching of Witness Lee for some years, and as we found out later, Gene caused no little disruption when he challenged Witness Lee's authority and ultimately broke away. Consequently, Gene was looking for a leaderless, floundering group like ours to take over and guide into the same type of church model that had been successful in China.

Somehow, Gene had heard of the Campus Crusade troubles, had known someone involved, and had made his way both to a group similar to ours in Goleta, California, a suburb of Santa Barbara, which was near the University of California at Santa Barbara, and to us in Eugene. At the time, I had the opportunity to build houses on the Oregon Coast, only an hour away, so I was not fully involved with the group on a daily basis as I had been for the previous two years. But I heard about what transpired.

Gene came and began speaking to the group. His passion and charismatic speaking ability gained their attention in addition to his supposedly advanced knowledge of God's word. He claimed to have esoteric knowledge from the Bible, implying he had inside information that others did not have. Under his influence, the group began meeting when Gene was there every night, and meetings did not shut down early.

My best friends began calling me, infatuated with their new member. "Terry, we think we've found the answer. Gene is here and teaching us."

"Who is Gene?" I asked.

"You've got to come hear him."

This was my social-spiritual group at the time, so of course, I did. We would gather early in the evening and sing favorite spiritual songs, all without any instruments, but we didn't need any. Our hearts were into it. We often stood in a large circle, arm in arm. It felt good, and we all enjoyed it very much. But when we otherwise would have stopped and gone home to bed, Gene began teaching. And he would go on until somewhere between ten thirty and midnight, or on occasion, one o'clock.

With a soft-cover Bible rolled up in his hand, he arose with purpose and passion, stabbing the air with the book for emphasis as he spoke. This got everyone's attention because we had been missing focus. Anyone with certainty and an ability to communicate as he did would certainly gain our hearing.

Eventually, Gene let it be known he stood in a chain of authority from the apostles through China because of his connection with Witness Lee and Witness Lee's with Watchman Nee in China. Witness Lee elevated the idea that the Chinese Church he came from was the true, hidden apostolic church, directly in line with the apostles of Jesus, although the evidence for this came from a veiled trail through history. Watchman Nee had ordained Lee as the new representative of Jesus Christ to the world. Gene, on the other hand, felt they had it wrong: He thought Witness Lee should appoint Gene to this role and place the baton in an American's hand, but Witness Lee disagreed. So a religious battle broke out, and Gene parted ways but still felt he was in a direct line with the apostles. And now, he had found us and felt we were his new people to lead to the gateway of heaven.

Gene did not talk about himself as the apostle of Jesus at first, but when he finally did, any signs of humility vanished. He indicated he was now the spokesperson for Christ on earth—I am not kidding. "If you do not know who I am by now," I heard him say one night to someone from the group who had a question—indicating we all should know he is the single representative of Jesus Christ for the world. He was like a Christian Dalai Lama, the Vicar (the word he used, traditionally reserved for the Pope as the representative on Earth) of Christ to the whole world. Had he introduced himself with that credential when he had first appeared, he would have had few, few followers.

My fellow spiritual seekers in Eugene were putty in the hands of a master religious salesman. Yet we were a forgiving bunch, to a fault. So this aspect of Gene was put to the side as perhaps an aberration. Because of my physical distance from the group and the fact I'd not been there from the start of his influence, I had a different view. His teaching was interesting, but his mysterious personality was puzzling. I think I had a more realistic perspective of what was happening. And I think he could feel my hesitancy about him.

As we've seen throughout time and still witness in all areas of life, we easily fall away from taking responsibility and let others do the thinking for us. In our religious settings, we find it convenient sometimes to let the denomination or the pastor or even the Bible tell us what to think. We follow because we think that we should. Or we follow what feels good at the moment without further consideration, relying fully upon good feelings and setting aside our abilities to analyze objectively.

Unfortunately, our Eugene group went with feelings and did little analysis. We were seeking our own way and to find our own faith but without any true leader. And although the heart of the group consisted of former Campus Crusade members, we had no one trained to do creative theological thinking. This was a new venture for everyone. Crusade staff was recruited without particular theological study directly from college campuses, as I was, and put into religious evangelism, straight to the A Team, bypassing the laborious—and thinking—work of seminary.

As mathematician, philosopher, and Harvard professor Alfred North Whitehead wrote, "In considering religion, we should not be obsessed by the idea of its necessary goodness. This is a dangerous delusion."

So, what happened to this group without the skill or desire to analyze whether someone, such as Gene, would truly benefit the group or not?

Initially, a leader fell into the hole we needed filling, and he showed us his way. Gene taught that he was there to find a special, few "called" people to climb the spiritual mountain to God, and when they got it just right, when their personal holiness reached perfection, and when they had home-style church life perking perfectly, they would wave up to heaven, and Jesus Christ would appear and descend back to earth to incorporate his worldwide kingdom. The group members Gene would designate as "called" would have unique leadership roles with Christ.

I could not buy into that, but by now, I had no influence with the group. However, I still cared about the people, and they respected and loved me, too, so I just hung around, quietly observing. I think Gene intuitively felt my resistance about him, although I had never said a word against him—I was just thinking. I didn't know what, if anything, was wrong. Something just did not feel quite right. So I was blown away one evening when I, one of Whitehead's naïve ones, who never thought a religious leader could step away from goodness to promote his own glory, fell under Gene's attack.

At this point, my book, *At Least We Were Married,* was flying off the shelves across the country, and they couldn't keep enough in print. Yet in our group, I was an ordinary person; I made nothing of the book, nor did anyone else. I was known as a simple "brother." But Gene, aware of my book status, evidently thought of me as an authority in the minds of the other members and a threat to his role as leader. And our group did not have room for two leaders.

In one of the meetings I attended, coming over from my home on the coast, we had so many present that we had to sit on the floor in the member's home to squeeze everyone into that packed room. In his talk, Gene made his way through the people on the floor and over towards me, paused, turned and looked back into the group, and swept his hand up and across everyone. Then he talked about a book he had written and discarded, implying the writing of books was self-exalting, foolish, and only fed a writer's ego. I felt his aim. This man knew what he was doing as he sent the subliminal message to the group that he was now taking over, and I could not stop him.

In a single act, Gene had both trimmed away a threatening authority figure and ensured no one would challenge him. His words had destroyed one of the most valuable tools in the world of freedom—books. If he could keep people from reading books by degrading them, the members would be stripped of their main channel for knowledge and some of their best outside resources to question him. So he did two things at once—destroyed my credibility and destroyed the value of books.

When the meeting ended, I walked out by myself into the dark, felt uneasy, and found my way back to the Oregon coast, just as I had after every other meeting there. I held no anger—but only because I had no idea what had hit me. Later, with time and reflection, as I put pieces together, I understood and saw into the invisible world of what Gene had done. I like to think it was one of my lessons in Spirituality 101—watch out for people who attach to your group and try to take over.

We all need to remain aware in our spiritual search for the enlightened path. In leaving ourselves open to finding "the" way, we leave ourselves also open to latching onto those with another agenda—feeding their ego at the expense of our spiritual search. We might want the spiritual happiness we long for so badly we take a short cut and, believing someone, like Gene, has the goods for us, we attach to that person. But we will only end up as trophy scalps for the person's collection of false power.

Despite what Gene did to me that night, I remained with the group, such as I could, while I continued living on the coast.

We numbered only about forty people in Eugene. But our friends in Goleta, California, by the University of California at Santa Barbara, had about one hundred fifty members. Gene was commuting back and forth between the two, staying for a few weeks at each place. We began to think it would be easier to have one group and wonderful to have a larger group. Whether Gene himself planted these seeds of thought or not, I do not know. But when he was gone, the whole group, including me, one Sunday afternoon in one of the member's living room, decided to move to Santa Barbara all as one and join the other group.

It did not take long. Our Eugene group picked up our stuff, rented U-Hauls, quit jobs or took leaves, and moved to California to be with other former national leaders in the campus organization who had relocated there, a beautiful place on the ocean.

I was finishing building a duplex, so I was the last to leave, about two months after the others. In the interim, although my best friend kept me somewhat informed, until I arrived, I had no idea what was going on with our merged group in California. In shock, I learned that before our Eugene group had moved to Goleta, Gene had just suddenly left. His departure without a word fell so far out of anyone's expectations or imagination that no one even broached the subject. And the Goleta group hadn't wanted to cause us any anxiety by telling us before our arrival that Gene had left, especially since they couldn't explain why.

We knew Gene was simultaneously working with the Goleta group, so we expected to see him there when we arrived; he was even more firmly entrenched as their leader than he was in our group. But it turned out Gene had silently taken off, mysteriously. He was gone, out of town, disappeared, in hiding somewhere—we weren't exactly sure, but his absence had a mysterious religious aura hanging over it. But no one knew where he was or when he would be back.

When I finally arrived in Goleta, people were working at new jobs and carrying on as normal. But there were no meetings, and no Gene. In Eugene, he had taught every night, which had helped to unify everyone, but now … nothing. And no one wanted to usurp his leadership position and start running any meetings, even if he had left.

When I got there, I got together with some from our Eugene group.

"What?" I said. "But why?"

"We don't' know—some say he is on a spiritual retreat."

"When will he be back?"

"No one knows."

Right away I thought of the parable of the lost sheep, that the good shepherd leaves all the ones who are safe and sound and goes out for the one lost sheep. For Gene to forsake the entire movement did not seem loving or like the heart of a spiritual leader. However, the expanded Goleta group itself seemed okay and would wait for Gene to return, although one or two families did eventually return to Eugene. But I was puzzled, and the academic-type detective in me would not be satisfied until I got to the bottom of it.

And I did, but not before Gene returned.

A couple of months later, Gene did come back, but quite secretly. He let it be known to his most devoted young people that he had disappeared to test everyone, to find out who would be faithful to him and "faithful to the Lord," equating the two—faithfulness to him meaning faithfulness to the Lord. There was another key to look for. People who identify their opinion, their mission, their view with the Lord's do so to keep others from even thinking about challenging them. Yet truth has the strength to stand up to challenges and leaves room for inquiry. People can figure out, question, doubt, come to their own understanding about whether what a leader says is of "the Lord."

I'm sorry to say, some people still followed Gene. Probably one third of the entire group went with him, although there was no way to know because it was done so secretly. One prominent family from Eugene followed Gene, and although we lived in the same town, we never saw one another or had a chance to speak to each other again. Gene discouraged personal contact with former friends.

But here is the good news about that family. Several decades later, the husband and father called from across the country to apologize to me, although it wasn't necessary. They had followed the man across the world for years, even helping to support him financially, only finally to figure out what Gene was really doing. It about destroyed him to realize the truth. He was bristling angry after spending his life following Gene. But better late than never. Each one of us figures things out in our own good time.

Sometime after Gene splintered the group, I found out why he had left. As it turned out, two older former national Campus Crusade leaders who had moved there to be part of the Eugene group—I'll call them Bill and Harry—precipitated Gene's leaving. When these two showed up and received attention and respect from all the young people because they had been national leaders in Campus Crusade, Gene felt stripped of his power. Gene was forty-two years old, and Bill and Harry were close to that age but a little younger. This clearly threatened Gene because he had taught that age has seniority in the church. He was still the oldest, but not by much. As I saw it, Gene had used his charisma and biblical slant to create a mask and costume for himself to cover his fear-based ego. And then feeling threatened when Bill and Harry arrived, his fear took over, and he took off. He was comfortable only surrounded with people who totally agreed to his preeminence. Furthermore, he appeared to be afraid of Bill and Harry and not willing to stand up to them face to face if need be.

Looking back, I can explain so easily what happened and why. But at the time, we could not see so clearly. Here was a group of young people, in the heart of our country's cultural revolution, wanting a special spiritual church life and thinking they'd found the way to get it through Gene. He had promised how it would be, and they had believed him. But, in reality, they had no training in how something like this could happen, no way to assess whether someone was leading them in the right direction, and no experience with such a leader in a religious movement having anything but good, pure motives.

His passion and the topics themselves—God, enlightenment, the way—seemed to leave no room for questioning for most members. And, although I did question him and his methods, I think he believed in what he was doing. After observing religious speakers of the passionate, absolutely certain type for several years, I have come to believe they embrace the philosophy they are presenting. The world is full of things which cause doubt, and we all like certainty—in it we find that most basic need for safety—and speakers of this type fill that void. Unfortunately, too many leaders in the religious world play upon this need and leave no room for healthy discussion of their methods and philosophy. With extremely high talent but inflated egos, they are looking for unsatisfied people seeking spiritual life. These would-be saviors may be anywhere in any religion and happily enlarge their power and false ego by wrapping others in their fold and telling them what to think.

One simple statement from Jesus encapsulates his evaluation of religion and its leaders: "By their fruits, you shall know them." How can we find the genuine good in religion? How can we find the path to spiritual reality? How do we know which spiritual leaders to follow? By looking at the fruit, the end-product, how people feel and act as a result of coming into that religion and under the influence of those leaders. Are the people happier, more fulfilled, more loving, closer to God in all senses of that phrase? Are they filled with greater compassion? Will they forsake their own safety to rescue one or more they feel can be rescued? Have they grown in maturity?

We certainly didn't reach any such highs from Gene's leadership. I still feel anger and disgust for him because of all the vulnerable people he led astray—and I continue to work on releasing those feelings. But I look at the larger picture and see what happened with Gene as contributing to my spiritual schooling. Every false, true, good, or bad experience can be used as a place to learn, to reflect, to grow, and to move forward stronger, wiser, and more compassionate than ever in one's previous life. So with Gene. What better way to learn these things than through experience? And for the multitudes who can't, what better way than to read a personal story like this one?

My experience with Gene did teach me valuable lessons. More than any, it taught me to get my own faith, use my own mind, and not allow any speaker, no matter how gifted, to inflate my ego in my spiritual search for enlightenment.

I learned that to degrade theological education and academic books leaves a person and/or group vulnerable to self-delusion, to teaching religion that might be entirely out of whack with truth. Education alone does not prevent this, but it does give people tools for evaluation.

Every group needs a leader, or it will degenerate into chaos or slowly melt away. And if the group does not appoint or elect a leader, often one will fill the gap on his or her own. This keeps the group together, but a danger comes when the group fails to acknowledge who is really giving direction; it leaves itself vulnerable to someone taking over who has a different agenda, especially one tied to ego-enhancement rather than the central purposes of the group.

Movements that think they are God's A Team, while everyone else is lost, are the most lost. Even my attitude that the church-pew warmers were somewhat spiritually dead set me up to follow a charismatic leader like Gene. I had to shift my entire viewpoint to one of grace—that the true people of God are those filled with the godly heritage, which is everyone.

All of this experience adds to my desire to look for and appreciate mature speakers who don't mind being disagreed with, who welcome goofy questions that challenge their authority, and who do not come across as super holy. They are out there, and I love and enjoy them and gain much from their insights.

I began this chapter looking for happiness and believing it would come through a spiritual experience with others. I learned, instead, that happiness was not the goal but the natural reward for a higher purpose.

So I learned that my story is not about happiness alone; it is about spiritual consciousness, although happiness comes with it. It reminds me of when we are thirsty. We seek water, and yet, at our feet, we might have something far better. If we concentrate on assuaging our thirst, we will pass up the gift lying before us—and only maybe find water. But if we let come what may, we will find the universe has something more powerful and fulfilling—and a cool, refreshing drink on the side.

Letting go of the quest for happiness is not easy. Most people think of happiness as our pot of gold at the end of the rainbow. But as long as we chase it, reach for it, and seek for it, happiness eludes us. Unfortunately, it's always just out of reach. But when we quit reaching for it, when we close our eyes and find out how to clear the clutter, how to speak a new language, how to think new thoughts and dwell on the good inside of us with gratitude … presto! We expand into a glorious, happy universe. There is spiritual enlightenment, holding out to us in its hand the happiness we thought was somewhere else. And it spills out into everything … if we let it.

CHAPTER 10

If at the end, when I come to lay down the reins of
power, I have lost every other friend on earth, I shall
at least have one friend left, and that friend shall be
down inside of me.

Abraham Lincoln

Lincoln's deep sense of integrity arose from within—knowing himself, knowing his beliefs, and knowing what thoughts and actions aligned with them. From that sound foundation, he could remain true to himself and make choices without regard to what others thought or said. We all, at some point, have to make tough choices. And if we stay in integrity, then we are honest and in tune with our real self and make the right decision, even if it does not match the opinions of others.

I, too, face my share of difficult choices and continue to work on remaining true to my spiritual principles. But one especially trying circumstance challenged me more than others, one concerning the subject of divorce.

"Terry," people asked, "did you ever get remarried?" It was the most common question I received once the book came out and I was speaking before groups. The answer then was no, but now is yes.

Jan was one of thousands who had moved up from the beaches of California to the green oak trees and valleys of Oregon to find community life on a simple basis. Through friends, she ended up finding our group in Eugene. I liked her. We had some common interests, especially trying to figure out what spirituality really was, and she was a perceptive listener.

In too short a time, we married and, not surprisingly, we had some problems from the start. Our few commonalities hardly made up for our differences. And we had never discussed some basic issues that most couples need to address before making commitments. We began with opposite, unidentified, and unspoken expectations, which presented some tough turf to cover right away.

In addition, although the wound in my heart with Nancy had healed a lot, a deeper one remained in the soul I didn't see. We had little in professional resources at that time to help people find their deeper wounds, and even if we would have, I found out that no magic potent can heal emotional wounds overnight. Wounds and grief from losing Nancy still lingered in my subconscious and ran very, very deep, so deep, in fact, even I did not know they were still there. Quite simply, I was not prepared for a new marriage.

Jan and I did well enough together, but after a number of years, our relationship just evaporated.

I am not sure I was a very good husband, although Jan would say I was in many ways. But she is generous. We can talk now and laugh together about our mistakes as we review them. We truly had a life of adventure for the years we were married. We have four wonderful children we truly adore and grandchildren, now, in the mix. And even though it was bumpy and then bumpier, Jan and I had some wonderful times, and I have no regrets.

But I came from a background where divorce was not even a topic for discussion. In my childhood home, the idea of divorce was considered so evil we weren't allowed to mention it. Such a seed planted in the mind of a child and nourished over the years grows strong into adulthood and can last a lifetime.

Voices dropped in our home whenever the word was used, say, at dinner when we heard of someone getting divorced, and the gloomy darkness surrounding the discussion gave the subtle message that we were touching upon a dark, sinful, and even mysterious subject. We were told you never, ever get divorced.

In my youth, a popular singer, Eddie Fisher, divorced Debbie Reynolds to marry her good friend Elizabeth Taylor. I was shocked in my naïveté, and my own heart felt crushed—my worldview was smashed. One of my heroes, Eddie Fisher, had turned into a bad man, which was my perception from my childhood programming. My perception and opinion were common for the times—NBC went on to cancel Eddie's TV show because of his divorce; that's how severely divorce was treated in those days. It was a considered a moral issue.

"Divorce is not an option," my parents agreed.

"You always work it out."

Right! Hardly.

I had a good home, and my parents were doing what they deemed the very best. If they had thought keeping a failing marriage intact would contribute to worse lives for their children, they would never have said such a thing. But that effort for good in my upbringing was actually contributing to making things not good for me as an adult.

At first, I held to the idea that if I tried hard enough, I could work out Jan's and my problems. But trying harder did nothing to help, and I couldn't fix our problems.

My upbringing had taught me that divorce was wrong, and by implication, divorced people were less worthy. Not surprisingly, when Christians divorce, many feel let down, damaged, wounded, betrayed, even guilty, and as a result, embarrassed. They might have been taught that since they have God in their lives when others don't, they have his special power to protect them from divorce. No wonder many feel defensive about their choice. People aim for perfection as a Christian, which, defined by their religion, includes marriage till death. Unfortunately, I carried those ideas with me from my childhood and had a tendency to look down upon people who were divorced— and I certainly didn't want to look down upon myself or give others reasons to see me in that light. I wanted to avoid divorce at all costs.

I also had heard the old slogan that "Christians who pray together, stay together." What I did not know were results of surveys by reputable professionals, like George Barna, who found that "divorce rates among conservative Christians were significantly higher than for other faith groups, and much higher than atheists and agnostics." Gulp! Why didn't someone tell us that?

At that time, many of the Protestant churches put a great emphasis on marriage with the expectation that the couple would get along perfectly and happiness would spread out. But nowhere in the Bible does it even suggest that for marriage.

It can help so many with their issues to realize that their faith does not make them perfect. And basing expectations on sanity and realism rather than on unfounded idealism can even promote healthier and longer lasting marriages. "It may be alarming to discover that born-again Christians are more likely than others to experience a divorce," the survey concluded back in the nineties. If only we had known.

Jan and I had problems, but we did the best at the time with who we were and what we believed. We were in the very heart of in the cultural revolution in America and the accompanying tumultuous religious upheaval, both of which allowed for more leeway in attitudes towards divorce. Yet, despite the changing times and revised values, I was still embarrassed when Jan and I did divorce. I had no desire to see anyone I cared about or respected for a while afterward. I hid out for a respite and time of personal reflection, and I needed to gain inner strength before facing the judgements of others.

The divorce experience was so extremely painful for me and a total last resort that I hit bottom. Just as losing Nancy to death was part of my process of advancing in my spiritual quest, so this experience, so contradictory to my self-image, had a similar effect. Divorce is also always a grief issue, and we go through the same steps in handling it as we do any other extremely emotional loss. As I worked through accepting myself for who I was—who I still was—I learned that if I was to attain higher spiritual consciousness, I needed to go through processes, and those generally take time. At least, getting over the downfall of my pride took time for me.

In coming to terms with how I saw myself after my divorce, I had to toss out blame. I had to stop attacking myself for doing wrong before I could love myself. And because love of self and others precedes spiritual consciousness, I realized I could attain that spiritual high only by breaking the habit of blaming—both myself and the other person.

Letting go of blame, however, does not excuse unloving behavior. We still take responsibility for our actions. We work to understand our mistakes and avoid them in the future. But we don't beat up ourselves or others over past misdeeds.

One reason churches were shocked at the divorce rates among church people is that divorced people tend to slip away and become unnoticed. Religious groups can become a club of sorts that give hidden messages that divorced people and others with problems are not completely welcome. They are suffering, they feel the subtle rejection of their church, and they retreat to themselves. Or, if they can, they move on to a church that does support them. We all need community support when we are in grief, and slipping away does not aid in the recovery process.

For me, however, my church fully supported me, which was a great lesson for me.

Over time as I worked through the issues, I learned that the divorce was better for us, and that was a hard pill to swallow. What I had thought—had been taught—at one time was evil, I now thought of as a good thing. That was hard, but it was part of my spiritual progression. I had to remain open, be willing to learn anew, and allow changes in my values and ideals if I were ever to attain my ultimate goal. If had not dealt with these issues, I would never be where I am today, which I feel is a very good place.

I am thankful Jan has grown as have I, and we have a better friendship than we ever had. The divorce allowed us to separate, get away from the negative focuses, and spend more energy on spiritual development. Having a higher purpose of the spiritual search allowed both of us to put the bad behind us. The Bible says, "I gave up childish things." Over the years, Jan and I have given up the childish behavior of harboring blame and guilt, seen more of the good in the other person, and kept the communication lines open. Both of us working on our spiritual development helps us to realize we are connected to something much, much bigger and higher, far beyond our temporal experiences here in this life, and we can give each other moral support.

Was the pain of the divorce worth it? Yes. Otherwise, one of us would have died of a stroke or high blood pressure. No kidding. Probably me first. We would not have the healthy lives we enjoy separately or the peaceful and supportive communication we give each other.

I knew an older person who had a miserable middle age and older life. She knew it and told me why.

"Terry," she said, "he ruined my life."

She had been divorced for many years, perhaps thirty by then, and still blamed her ex for her misery in all the ensuing years. This does not make sense to me. She had let that one thing in her far past affect the rest of her life with a poisonous attitude. What a waste! Life is now and ahead; the past has been lived and is gone.

I do not necessarily recommend divorce. Honestly, does anyone ever get divorced just for the fun of it? No, and it is never fun.

But I also do not necessarily advocate staying in a loveless marriage.

Staying married or getting a divorce is a personal decision, and different situations can justify one or the other. Considerations of children's well-being, health-care coverage, financial stability, and more can determine what one chooses. It all depends, and each person when faced with a marriage that no longer works needs support to weather the trials ahead.

Many of us expect that kind of support to come from our churches, but too often, we find none. Churches readily comfort when their members grieve over the death of loved ones. But the loss of a marriage—not only of a partner but also of the hope-filled expectations—results in an equally hard-hitting grief, often made worse by religions holding back on the much-needed comfort.

The opinions of others could have no bearing on my choosing what was best for me, as it turned out. I had to listen to my own soul's voice, not the little voice played out from childhood programming. As difficult as I found that process, I recognize that it advanced me in my spiritual search because it forced me to go into myself to get my own answers more clearly and trust God was leading and guiding me. In the end, I found staying true to myself, believing in my own goodness, and keeping my spiritual goal foremost in my mind allowed me to make the best decision with confidence.

CHAPTER 11

*What man actually needs is not a tensionless
state, but rather the striving and struggling for a
worthwhile goal.*

Viktor Frankl

Victor Frankl sounds as if he read my life story.

Going the unconventional route is built into my DNA, and it has created tension—especially until I learned simply to surrender to life and trust it. However, strain still comes with striving for a higher goal. Like climbing one of the rocky Alps, we can't avoid the struggle—looking up to the far-off summit, seeing thousands of feet down where we've traveled, holding on for dear life to whatever we can grasp, turning from the biting onslaughts, hoping the partners we're roped to can carry their share, while through it all, feeling so alone.

Sometimes, I felt the temptation to avoid the struggle. I would ask myself, "Why not wise up and take the normal route, go the way most people do? Go to work every day. Take my two weeks' vacation, maybe later three. End up with a nice retirement, if I live long enough."

But whenever I tried to be "normal," blend in, be like everyone else, and live an ordinary life, I didn't feel right. I was fighting myself. I could just as well die; being normal was so much against the personality I brought into the world. I am individualistic and want to see for myself what works. In the world of religion, I challenged everything, seeking to unlock the doorway into the spiritual world—above us, around us, beneath us, and especially, in us.

Even if we live an ordinary life, if we don't test our beliefs and question our activities to some degree, try things, learn to think for ourselves, we simply slink down and coast with the masses and end up taking whatever the world gives us—through the government, the corporation, the stock market, the job, the church, the schools, or whatever. Our seventy to ninety-five years slip by, and the next thing you know, we are gone. It is as true for me as for everyone. And what will I leave as a legacy? What is my purpose and mission in the world? The spellbinding thing for me as I look back now, is that I was right on with my mission through all the tension, striving, and struggling Victor Frankl talks about.

During all the turmoil around the group in Goleta, California, I remained true to myself, and as I continued searching and questioning, this kept me on my spiritual path. The time after Gene left us represents a major progression in that journey.

After most of our Eugene group saw the failure of the larger Goleta group's efforts and returned home to Oregon and a few continued to follow Gene, I remained in California. So did a fairly large remnant of the original Goleta group. But they felt lost, in a sense. Like me, they had nowhere to go, no place to belong, and were scattered around the various apartments and duplexes in Goleta in no identifiable group. Before long, several of us began to get together to study and discuss what we might do next, and so I did with other men in the early mornings and most evenings

We were seventies people, and few of us would ever fit back into ordinary life. As the dust settled in the country—the Viet Nam war was winding down and the counterculture was settling into the background—we lacked a big cause to rally around. Janis Joplin sang to us about leading our own lives and not giving personal power over to anyone anymore. Frank Sinatra's "My Way" continued to resonate in the hearts of the people, the heart of the culture, and certainly in our spiritual search.

But what exactly did it mean to lead our own lives? We hadn't a clue. We leftovers in Goleta were still not driven by money or material riches. We sought the deeper riches, like peace in the world, love between people, and justice. But how? Our goal in Goleta had been to find the knowledge of God for the mix and how to live that out in a compassionate community, and we were left standing short.

And some of our beliefs actually prevented us from advancing in our goal. For instance, our movement in both the Eugene and Goleta groups devalued higher education, especially in theology. No one in Campus Crusade or the house church movement had challenged that ideal, so we couldn't turn to a seminary or a theological institution for added and professional knowledge about how to accomplish what we were trying to do. Anyone going to a formal graduate school for greater knowledge of God, the Bible, or theology was suspect. For this movement, it would be almost as if the person were capitulating to the enemy.

As you might guess, a fellow who follows his own path doesn't forever stick to such limiting rules, and I didn't. Nor did I see books and learning as impediments to spiritual advancement—just the opposite. And fortunately, my daily work schedule allowed me time to delve into reading.

To provide during this time, I was now working in construction. It was fun, actually, to get out on the job with the construction guys, stretch our muscles, and build massive concrete college buildings or condos or a freeway bridge hundreds of feet above the canyon bottom.

Breaks on the job gave me a little time to study the Bible. Early mornings and evenings were taken up with meetings in Goleta to discuss what to do next and examine the Bible for new insights, and on my own, I had even begun to study church history.

The people scattered around Goleta who had placed their hopes in a spiritual community now found that was all gone. So we soon decided to have one more try. As our new efforts began in Goleta, within one square mile, we now had two groups trying to be the exemplary, new-church-development model—Gene's and ours.

As we were spending these months meeting and discussing a plan, Bill and Harry were still in Goleta and wanted to give another go at building a church community. I had known them for seven or eight years by then and knew they both had good hearts. But the people would not trust them. Gene had degraded them, and people were reticent to listen to them now. It turned out the two wanted to include me in their leadership group so I could help bridge the age gap. I was younger than they were, and they told me that having me in the leadership group would help with their credibility. I didn't know why, truthfully. I was rather quiet, not quick to voice opinions, and fairly gentle with people. I thought at times I should be more vocal and tougher with people, but they felt the people liked me.

Initially, a few of us met mornings at five o'clock at a Holiday Inn for a butter horn and coffee and to study the Bible for new direction. About a dozen men usually showed up. We were trying to brush aside our previous ideas about the Bible and look at things in a new way. This willingness to challenge our own assumptions represented a huge change for me and, without my realizing it at the time, pushed me forward on my path to higher consciousness. It also fit in with my tendency to go against the norm, and I would carry this value forward with me.

We asked, for example, if the word "gospel" means "good news" and if it was so good, why was the gospel we believed not working to make things better? Why were churches so moralistic, so legalistic, trying to be everyone's conscience and moral guide? Why were they out of date in style and theology? Why were they boring? Why did they pull the devil out of the backroom to scare kids into repenting?

We read some of the early church writers and made enlightening discoveries. We found the groundwork for the Roman Catholic Church, the mother church of the West. We encountered Eastern scholars and found ways of looking at the gospel we had never considered.

In our early morning studies, we learned the formation of the Bible came later than the events it describes. This seems so obvious now, but the way we were taught to read the Bible did not include much consideration for these kinds of issues. Even as a young person, I always wondered how the early church got along if the Bible was so important because they did not have a Bible. It hadn't been written yet.

We finally felt free to ask questions, and they just poured out. I, especially, reveled in the opportunity to give vent to ideas that had been brewing in the back of my mind. We were examining our faith for ourselves and questioning the beliefs that were handed to us. For me, this experience was invigorating. I could hardly wait to get up in the mornings, get to the Holiday Inn, and meet with the guys. Others in the group, however, lost interest after a while, and the original twelve or so eventually dwindled to only three of us: the former Campus Crusade leaders, Bill and Harry, and me. Still, we met every day, and this went for about a year.

In working on forming the church community, our Goleta remnant group experimented with different ideas but usually encountered only frustration. We would try one style of organization, meeting, teaching, or structure; find out it didn't work; and so we'd move on and try another.

One skill we never bothered to develop was to make decisions based upon a consideration of everyone's intuitions and feelings. Crusade had steeped us in the authoritarian model of leadership from the top, and we did not realize there could be a different style, which would be to look to the people themselves and hear what they were hearing and see what they were seeing and bring it all together with our feelings and thoughts. So we continued in the old way—getting the ideas and execution of those ideas from the top and dismissing the suggestions of the others. For example, one of the members was always excited and every week had a new idea. He got a reputation as being "a doctrine of the week guy," said in a pejorative way to indicate he was wasting everyone's time, and lost his credibility; no one bothered to listen openly to him.

Our repeated attempts to create the ideal church community continued to go nowhere, and I began to feel that the blind were leading the blind. I think we got as far as we could get without having—or, better, getting—the proper tools to narrow our experiments. Our attitude toward academic learning hindered our advancement and limited our possibilities. We weren't fluent in the original Bible languages so we could analyze the writing only as far as the translations allowed us. We did not respect scholars at universities who had devoted their lives to the same questions we were asking, so we could not benefit from their insights. And the results we got did not come near to satisfying us. I felt as if our attempt at creating a church community was standing on shaky ground.

I also felt more and more uncomfortable about Harry who seemed to be taking over. He was forceful but also rough. I knew from my experience in recovering from the accident that, regardless of good intentions, insensitive treatment does not work with people. Telling me, as that one man had done as I lay in the hospital, that the devil "had done it" did not aid in my healing. Instead, treating others with respect and sensitivity creates a much better foundation for working cooperatively with them.

Harry seemed to be stepping over from firm to harsh in his treatment of others more and more often with only counterproductive results. I suspect he anxiously wanted positive results, and as they continued to elude us, he manifested more anxiety in a fiercer, angrier, more controlling persona. One evening I remember in particular, Harry asked me to accompany him to the apartment of a young woman who had been part of our group at one time and, now, with the others who had come to Gene's meetings earlier or even one of ours, had scattered around Goleta. We hadn't seen her in a while and wanted just to say hello, to keep our door open, so to speak. She was a college student at the University of California at Santa Barbara and had the quintessential Southern California look—long, shiny, natural blond hair and light sun-tanned skin.

We dropped by her apartment unannounced, which was not uncommon in Goleta, an informal college town.

"Are you with us or against us?" Harry demanded of her, once we got inside and stood across her dining room table.

I stood by, amazed at the combative tone to his words. "Wait a minute," I thought. "Where is this coming from?" I felt she needed defending against him, and I almost jumped into the conversation. His words and tone had set me off. And when that happens, I usually keep my feelings inside until I've had time to think the situation over. I don't like to say something that erupts in me and regret it later. So, even though I was furious, I kept my mouth shut so I could think this over more completely.

"Well …," she hesitated.

"Hey," he said, "it's our way or the highway. You are either in or out."

These were his exact words, and I can see the setting as clearly at this moment as then. And the tightness and shock and embarrassment—for her, for me, for our group—I felt then still stirs in me as I remember his attacking words.

"I can't say," she stumbled.

"Okay, you're out," he said and left her in tears as we walked out.

I felt betrayed. Not by the young woman but by this colleague. At first, I thought maybe I was overreacting. After all, he was older and acted as if he knew more. But I remember walking to the car, and something in my gut said this was terribly wrong. I continued to keep quiet, but finally I said, "Do you think that might have been a bit strong?"

Harry gave no immediate reply, but as he started up the car, he told me that we don't need people like her around. Not surprisingly, we never did see the young woman again.

I know I got quiet after he said that, and I kept my feelings to myself for the moment. But this girl's boundaries had been invaded; she had been wronged. That night, Harry had not honored her as a human being with the freedom of her own choices. He had violated her basic right to think for herself and take whatever time that took. It started to feel as if we had jumped from one bad deal into another—from the problems with Gene to now this. Everyone who took charge acted with authority, which we needed, but each took it too far. Intent on doing only what they thought right, our leaders didn't listen to the people and became rough, stomping on anyone in their way.

My bad experience that evening was certainly an uncomfortable moment, but it began opening my eyes to a new view of what was happening around me. Maybe living in the turbulence of the country then helped: My own new values were emerging as the times were changing. I saw that uniformity was becoming the new religious rule Harry and Bill were promoting, and I was not in step with them. We were reverting to old—and too familiar—ways: Uniformity was the way everyone was expected to operate in Campus Crusade as well as under Gene, and now, even though we had parted ways with them, we were back the same style. Authoritative rule and expectations of conformity left no room for people to do their own thinking. As I saw the unfortunate results of this practice, I learned to remain alert to avoid later any religious group that demands uniformity of thought and behavior of its members.

I knew that the incident with the Santa Barbara student was not the end of the story; more would follow. What started off bad, grew exponentially worse as more people came under their verbal attacks. They were not respecting individuals, leaving no room for opinions different from their own.

These experiences fed into my growing questioning of the norm. They helped me see the dangers of uniformity of thought, that the worst side of religion is exposed when the goal is mindless thinking, or really, no thinking at all by the members—where everyone is taught to think and believe exactly the same. Instead, with an open window of thought and belief, everyone has healthy space to grow into his or her own faith. But at the time, when this entire experience was completely new to us, I did not know whether to trust my head or my heart—my heart told me we were rushing to a dead-end disaster and I should bail out now, but my head said we had a good goal so I should stay and work through this problem.

Meanwhile, I felt our group was wandering even farther from its intent. We had a goal but had no idea how to reach it, and our attempts were just collapsing in on us. We tried meeting in different homes and even had rented a large building in the middle of the campus community of the University of Santa Barbara, and nothing in that regard made any difference. We tried passing the torch around for speaking and teaching, but that cut out any chance for continuity. We tried using the only model we had, the old Crusade one for worship, which was singing and a talk. But the people did not like singing anymore. By now, quite a few children were running around, which contributed to a sense of bedlam and disorganization. And people were complaining about complaining because we had no effective system to deal with problems—listening and validating others' perspectives.

Eventually, after a year or so, the church settled into about fifteen family groups. We had created six deacons, but because they did not know what was going on either, their style of leadership was defensive and hard-nosed, just like Harry's. I did not have the authority or the knowledge to do much about any of this, only the insight that it was not working well. And I felt no one could—or wanted to—stop our wild trajectory. We were speeding down the icy hillside like a runaway bobsled towards the cliff.

This work I had been involved with since leaving college was not bearing good fruit. For a moment, I thought about leaving and starting a group of my own there in Goleta, but I didn't consider that for long. I realized how stupid that would be. We would have a town split into three groups, not two, and who was I to think I would do any better?

I looked back on these years associated with the Crusade groups to pull together what I had gained and, maybe, gain clues about my next step. I'd learned some tough lessons.

I had worked in church evangelism, the best, and understood it. But I gave it up because I saw its weaknesses and knew there had to be a better way. I learned to look for results in religion and not focus on the fine points of its doctrine.

I learned the traditional Western church doctrines that some held sacred had weaknesses. I didn't know enough to know which ones and what they needed.

I had tried to build a church based on the first century model. But I gave it up because it did not serve modern-day needs. Some people love antiques, but they are mostly showpieces, not practical for daily use. That is what the earliest church became for me. Interesting. Thought provoking. Educational. Historically fascinating. But certainly not a practical model.

I had allowed a person with passion and force to lead a group and tell us what to think. But I gave up relinquishing control because power given to another destroys those who stop questioning.

I had thought a few others had a special connection God and could help me find the way to him. But I gave that up because I saw that their insecure egos got in the way of sharing equally among all and I knew that God excludes no one.

Having put my work with Campus Crusade and its offshoots behind me, I felt very much on my own. What options remained for me?

I did consider settling down to an ordinary life and getting a job, but that idea didn't last for long. I thought of taking my home building/development business to a higher and more successful level, but that was just not in my heart and would not have worked for me or my personality. I was still a spiritual entrepreneur, an explorer and an adventurer, and I sincerely desired to work through the lab of religion and spirituality.

I felt I had a great role model for both going my own way and incorporating spirituality into my life. The ultimate entrepreneur, Jesus, broke the molds of his culture, the Bible at that time, and the morals of his day. He followed his own law, God's law for him at that time, and continually broke the religious or Roman laws. But he always had a good defense—that what he was doing was good for people.

I had another role model for independent thinking and spiritual searching close to me. Having grown up Lutheran, I knew about Martin Luther, the sixteenth-century reformer, who had followed his own path and, despite extreme pressure to lay aside his views contrary to the Catholic Church, had stuck to it. To have disagreed with the church as he had, I thought, he must have had a unique understanding of the Bible. If I could find out what he had believed and taught, I might get fresh information.

Thus, my quest for a theological system that would work for me now had more definition: Which theological system gives us the power to be the person of love-compassion as Jesus and others taught? What system lets us overcome guilt at the gut level, live in peace and harmony as an automatic reflex, grow in strength to overcome frustration, rejection, worry, and anxiety? Just as important, what gives us permission to fail, make mistakes, and still be spiritual?

These are the questions I was asking myself in Goleta after I saw the failure of our groups and as I began learning to break the traditional, conventional mode. Even though I tended to go my own way, I still held onto many beliefs, systems, routines engrained in me in my upbringing. So, opening myself to new ways—getting outside the box with fresh questions and trying to gain alternative answers to life's questions—took time and determination.

My quest was by no means over; I was still searching. I thought back to that night in the hospital when Nancy died. I had had such a high spiritual experience, as though Nancy herself had been with me and guiding me. It had been like rising into a new heavenly dimension of reality, so I knew there was something better in life to be had. I knew it would be in the context of others, participating in a group or church. But where would I find it? I had no idea.

An ancient Chinese wisdom says, "When the student is ready, the teacher appears." That doesn't necessarily mean a literal teacher but, rather, that when the mind is ready for new learning, the opportunities for the perfect lessons will arise. After some nine years revolving around Crusaders—following the Crusade win-the-world model, working on the vision for a community church model, and coping with people around me clamoring for authority and leadership—while I searched for a higher spiritual consciousness I couldn't quite define, a next important step appeared just ahead on my path.

CHAPTER 12

*Of all religions, Christianity is without a doubt the
one that should inspire tolerance most, although, up
to now, the Christians have been the most intolerant
of all men.*

Voltaire
Eighteenth Century Philosopher

I was still living in California, in the Santa Barbara suburb of Goleta,
supporting myself as a carpenter in construction, now as a foreman.

In my free time, I had been gathering books from garage
sales in Santa Barbara, mostly having to do with religion, and already
a small library over a desk in my bedroom had begun to form. It felt
as if I was moving in tune with nature, like the squirrels in the forest.
Back in Oregon, from the window where I had written my book, I
had watched them gather nuts and dig down under the falling leaves
to bury and hide their treasures for the coming cold and scarcity of
the winter. They do it instinctively, without thinking. Likewise, I was
accumulating books, somewhat instinctively, with no defined purpose.

One evening, I had some free time and was moving along like
nature, without thinking of anything in particular, perusing my books,
when a thought from the background of my mind emerged and then
settled in, nudging me along. I had been reading those old books
(and I still have some of them) and learning ideas about how people
develop churches and what they believed, and I was beginning to feel
that formal study in a traditional graduate school setting, possibly
seminary, could be the thing our Goleta group needed, that someone
should do it, and that I was probably that someone.

We likely would not need to travel far to start formal study. There in Santa Barbara, one of the most beautiful small cities in America, stood Westmont College, an independent evangelical college, which had assembled a first-class library.

One day, when I was between jobs in construction, I decided to drive over and check out Westmont's library. I told no one my plans because I wanted to browse and see what I might bump into. I was primarily interested in theology.

As I headed out onto the freeway entrance from Goleta that next morning, it was a bit foggy, typical of the Santa Barbara climate. The report was that it would clear up and hit about seventy degrees later, typical also. The season was late fall, but one would never know it as the four seasons are all alike on that point, a hundred-some miles west of Los Angeles. Leaves don't turn, and there is never a smell of fall in the air, both of which I had missed during my three years in the area. But the year-round temperate climate and beautiful setting more than made up for what it lacked.

I parked my Westphalia VW camper in the lot at the north end of the Westmont campus and followed a map over a walkway, bordered by neatly trimmed green grass, which I can still see in my mind's eye, and found the library. Downstairs on the main-level entrance, they had tables and a few books, but the main stacks were a level above, at the top of a wide staircase. Above me, I could see stacks and stacks of books.

Only a few students were using study carrels, I was surprised to notice. It may even have been a break. So it was wonderfully silent, like an empty church at midnight.

I found the theology section upstairs over to the right of the landing and began to peruse the stacks, slowly walking up and down the aisles. My fingers were scanning across the covers of some of the books as I slowly shuffled my feet along. I found a book here and there I would take to a study carrel for fifteen or twenty minutes to look over more closely. I wasn't searching for anything in particular. I didn't think, just browsed, pulling a book off and seeing what was interesting. It was like walking along the beach with an eye out for driftwood or seashells—nothing in particular—just meandering along. We never know what our unconscious mind is feeding into us, however.

All of a sudden, I stumbled across a large set of maroon, hard-bound, prominent-looking books, taking up eight or ten feet of shelf space, perhaps fifty or sixty volumes, which instantly drew my attention. When I saw the author, the books completely pulled me in. The name on the cover shocked me—I had no idea books such as these existed even though I had grown up Lutheran. These books contained the writings of *the* Martin Luther, the monk of the six-teenth century—the one the civil rights leader and his father, Martin Luther King Sr., had been named after. This Luther, the reformer, had changed the world nearly five hundred years earlier with his radical but well-thought-out ideas. I had been thinking about the name of this man and wondering what he stood for. What were these books doing in this evangelical library?

Later I found out these were just a portion of his books in translation from the original German and Latin. I had grown up in the evangelical wing of the Lutheran Church when education and theological probing was not done much in the local churches. I had not been exposed to these books, or even anything about Luther's academic background. No one ever taught us that Luther was a scholar, an intellectual university professor, a prolific writer, and that his writings were available for us.

I slid out a couple of volumes and made it to my study car-rel. When I opened the book—and it didn't matter what volume or page or subject—the words fairly leaped off the sheet and through my eyes. It was as if a message of fire was burning at me, telling me to pay attention.

I have had too many such synchronistic experiences not to believe the great universe has moments prepared for us if we happen to be ready for them, special moments in the great mind of God to direct us into our life's purpose. Although sometimes, I get lazy and miss them, I watch for them, and always, they lead me in the direction I need to go. Each new day fills me with excitement as I wonder what wonderful synchronistic events will guide me on my journey.

Discovering those books changed my life, and I knew something extraordinary had happened to me, as if a door I had not seen before suddenly had sprung open to reveal a vista of untold beauty. And yet, my mind quietly took in the moment, like a blank whiteboard receiving colors and writings. I suddenly realized that the speakers and teachers in the movement I had given my life to over the previous years, from Campus Crusade through to our house church efforts, had misled me. Luther was not a lucky monk who stumbled into the Reformation, as they had suggested. Instead, I saw on the pages clear, incisive, and decisive words of strength and wisdom. I was stunned. The connection I felt with Luther at that moment stands as one of the most highly captivating and spiritual experiences of my life, and it gave hints that there might be a touchstone I could relate to in jump-starting my spiritual journey now gone dead.

Not everyone knows the importance and value of Martin Luther the Reformer in the history and life of the world, and I didn't, either, at the time. He is so intriguing that, according to *Time* magazine's October 31, 1983 issue, commemorating Luther's five hundredth birthday, more books have been written about Martin Luther than any other man in history except for Jesus. Luther's influence extended beyond the Lutheran Church: All denominations of Christianity and even other religions worldwide were utilizing the results of his work and writings. Although, at the time, I didn't realize the impact Luther had made, I sensed a wondrous treasure had revealed itself to me.

Maybe you have heard the story of the man who sold his land and traveled the world in search of diamonds. Upon his return, impoverished, he found the new owners of his property rolling in riches. They had noticed the sparkling stones in their creek, and behold, they found the property was rich in diamonds. It had been under the former owner's feet all along, but he had never noticed, had never bothered to look, and had assumed his fortune lay else-where. Well, I, a Lutheran, had stood on acres of diamonds and didn't know it. Because the Lutheran Church no longer represented Martin

Luther's theology, his writings and others' discourses about him had remained hidden from me in my religious upbringing. I had no idea of the extent of the literary works about this man. Later I learned that, on average, six hundred books and articles from across the world are written about Martin Luther *every year*.

Back at the library stacks at Westmont, I was starting to see the sparkles in my discovery. Because the books were on a lower shelf, I knelt down and pondered what was before me. As I looked over the whole collection and prepared to leave for the day, it never occurred to me that God was speaking to me, but he was. I only knew I was having a powerful, spiritual moment. The Divine itself was radiating a powerful energy as I opened these books. The feeling was less but similar to what I had felt in the hospital hallway that night Nancy was killed. So intensely did I experience the Divine that, there, in that library, I made the decision to apply for education at a Lutheran seminary. I got home later that day and began composing my letter to the seminary to get an application.

There was no turning back. When I returned to my small library and pondered my experience, I knew something had changed in me. I had new and fresh hope for my life's journey. The experiment I had been having in Eugene and now in Goleta was to be over for me. If I was to be of help to these people, I had to go away, gain what I could through education, and return to share my discoveries.

I spent the next few weeks pondering what I had experienced in the Westmont library. I also pondered what was happening there in Goleta with the people, and the church experience experiment we'd been searching to attain. To go back to the Lutheran Church would be going against everything we believed—that those organized churches were dead.

I thought to myself, never speaking of these things to anyone, that perhaps the way we had disdained the organized churches might be unfair. Maybe I should give it a try and see from the inside. I also thought that there were people in those churches like me, wanting more of God, remaining open to change, and needing help and leadership.

Once I received information back from the seminary, I applied rather quietly. A Lutheran seminary of the Norwegian heritage, it had more of a classical emphasis because I wanted to get the historical, classical message clear in my mind before moving forward into more experimental and progressive theological endeavors. To get in, I had to take Graduate Record Examination (GRE) and was accepted into the seminary in Minnesota. Only then did I let my friends know.

Meanwhile, the system in Goleta had become so authoritarian that some leaders were telling the people that they could not make any decisions without submitting it to the leadership. This included buying a house, getting married, getting a job, spending money, and so on. I was finding this distasteful and way off direction from our original vision.

Still, their extremely negative reaction to my decision to leave for the seminary surprised me. If we truly sought God and truth, which is what I thought we were doing, why would we not be open to one of our own who brought something back from God to us?

Later, I thought of Socrates, murdered by his own people he was trying to release from spiritual blindness. His fellow Athenians had preferred to stay blind than to see. And I thought of his famous story of the myth of the cave where the blinded people murdered the prophets who came to heal them, release them, and let them see the fullness of life in the light.

What I was doing was taking steps of new faith into newer faith all the time. Even the disciple Paul taught that there is no single final faith we achieve but that life is going from faith unto faith. If my story reveals anything, it is about constantly moving forward, never standing forever on the ground we've gained, but continually building more vision, more tools for accomplishment and conquering and gaining greater faith in the life of the Spirit of God. Ultimately, I came to believe that God gives us faith, not to get to a point where we simply rest on what we have gained, enjoy our accomplishments, and retire into frivolous activities but, rather, to keep applying all we can in our spiritual growth so that it builds until the day we die.

I felt that if I had submitted my leaving for the seminary for approval I would have been considered a traitor just by asking. What did they fear? How did merely making a suggestion threaten them? Did they have such a tenuous faith that it could not stand even questioning a new idea? Not surprising, by this time, I was no longer participating in some of the leadership decisions because I was not feeling good about the process. I knew I had to think for myself and act for myself, and I actually felt good about it.

In Goleta, I got together with Bill, who had some seminary education, and let him know what I was doing. At first, he was truly excited for me. Later, once some of the others spoke up against my decision, he shifted. He did not always follow through with his own heart and mind and could give in to someone he thought was stronger.

Then I went from surprise to shock.

Have you ever been under someone's wrath? As a child, maybe; but as an adult? But I was no one's kid any longer. When Harry got wind of my decision, he got angry, like a snake rising from the grass. "Angry" understates his reaction; he blew his top and found words beyond what any sailors ever used. I'm glad I wasn't there when he did this. Once I got a better education in psychology, I learned that people who are weak and get angry a lot use the threats of their anger to control others. Just so with this man: It helps them cover their deep insecurity and provides a feeling of power. He used his anger to the T. But he would not control me, and I was not afraid of him. That exacerbated him and really put me on the outside with those afraid of his wrath.

One would have thought I had turned into the devil's father himself. Isn't it interesting how someone can be an angel one moment, and suddenly, when he decides not to dance to the piper's tune any longer, he is a demon? All I needed was a red suit and a pitchfork to make me complete. As I reflected later, I realized that the group had fallen into mass control, and if I, a respected member, was allowed to make my own decision and leave with blessing, the two men leading the group would lose everything. Ultimately, my leaving did break open the minds of others, and the group disintegrated.

Despite the negative feelings arising from this, I was glad for the experience. It clarified in my mind what kind of spirit the group had fallen into and made it easy to move. Unity had come to mean uniformity, and I already knew that uniformity was not a tenet of a healthy human life group.

They could no longer control me, but they still had a grip on the other members. In a meeting called without me, the leaders told the others that anyone seen talking to me would be thrown out of their church. I was bad. But if it was obvious that I was so bad, why couldn't the other members be allowed to see for themselves? Evidently, I was poison and might infect them as well.

I had felt the leadership of this group getting more and more wacky, but I didn't realize how close it was to going off the deep end. The leaders felt threatened. The people were my friends, but they felt caught in the middle because they still found value in the group, and to talk to me, they had to slip over after dark or make a quiet phone call. Sounds immature of the leaders, doesn't it? And it was.

I thought back to times in history when the church itself hauled people off to burn at the stake, to behead, or to throw into dungeons. It always acted in the name of righteousness—whether it was hanging witches, burning heretics at the stake, or hauling innocent fathers and mothers to prison for reading their Bible and praying at home. And who had led these inhumane activities? Leaders in the churches and super-leaders. Can it help but remind us of the story of how religious leaders instigated the arrest, false trials, and crucifixion of Jesus of Nazareth? But those stories came from centuries ago. Does the church, sometimes, now turn into the spirit of the very ones who crucified the one they call their Lord?

In my naïveté, in this time before widespread terrorism, I thought our civilized society had truly put such acts of hatred and violence in the name of religion behind it. Or at least Christianity had. After all, the founder of Christianity, Jesus, had taught us to love even our enemies.

But had Christianity put those practices or similar ones away for good? Or could the "righteous" in the community, once again, lead the "faithful" to brutality as they had in the witch-hunts and the Inquisition and during the Crusades? Could that mentality rise again?

My quest, my Holy Grail, called for building a connecting bridge within myself between the vast, invisible spiritual universe, filled with God, and the visible, concrete earth in which I was born and now live. Religion claimed to be that bridge between God and earthlings. But how could we believe that when religions became so violent and destructive? How could I accept any religion if it had such a dark side to it? My experience in Goleta was giving me vital knowledge of what those persecuted people must have felt. I wasn't just reading about what had happened; I was living it in modern times, almost as if I were going back in history and experiencing those errant church behaviors myself.

Isn't the issue the same? Protection of the power of the righteous hierarchy over the "sinful body of unclean" people against an independent thinker who breaks free?

I clearly felt the hatred from Bill and Harry and sensed how, without society's controls, it could feed into violence. Had this been another time in history and another place, under different laws, under a more politically powerful church, they would have tried to destroy me physically in some way. It is the only time in my life I felt this kind of threat. My going my own way threatened the authority of the two and their hold on the whole group. And their egos were wrapped up in both. If I thought on my own, others might. If my independent thinking resulted in my leaving, others might leave. And if too many left, where would Bill and Harry be? Their entire identification lodged in the success of that group, and I was destroying their group.

As shocked as I was by their behavior, I held no anger. Despite all the extreme reactions and childish behavior surrounding my decision, I was too determined in my new direction to let this evil stuff stop me. Too many things had lined up to show this was the spiritual direction for me. I had been in the habit of reading the Bible daily since I was eighteen years old, so it did not take long to see the bigger picture of what was happening and why I was being treated the way I was. Weak, insincere people who needed to have control over others to feel personal validation were feeling their very existence threatened. They may have looked strong and powerful when up in front, preaching or teaching, but down inside, they were weak as a wet noodle.

I remembered that, historically, people seen as common sinners were never the butt of this kind of treatment from religious authorities. Instead, those in charge focused on the truly righteous, the people who were connecting to God in humble faith. They threatened the power of those in control because the closer to God we get, the more personal freedom we feel and the less we can be controlled or threatened by anyone, especially the self-righteous who try to dictate people's right to ultimate freedom and joy in life.

One wonders who the real villains are in the world.

Looking back, I might say to myself that I should have known this all along. But I had thought all of us in the group wanted the same thing, which was higher spirituality. So I had overlooked some of the differences as long as I could for the greater good.

My shock came from realizing how far our goal had slipped from us; I'd had no idea. And I felt sorrow for some of the people I cared about. But I began to realize if they wanted to stand up they would have to get their own courage and fight their own battles. My path was taking me in another direction.

Having been accepted to seminary in Minnesota, I put my house up for sale, bought a truck, loaded it up, and prepared to drive away to seminary. But I had to take a detour. My dad was in the Goleta Valley General Hospital, following heart surgery in Santa Barbara, and I remained in the area to visit him.

Several weeks had passed since I had moved out, but I was still in Santa Barbara, and two of the members from Goleta called and asked if they could talk to me on Sunday afternoon in the hospital lobby. These were fine individuals, who had grown up in the Southern California area and were both now working for IBM. I met them, and we walked down to the hospital cafeteria. I had no idea what they wanted but was always open to discussion

They said, "Terry, we want you to know we made a really bad mistake."

"What happened?" I asked.

"When the guys came to us, they said stuff that made you look really bad, that you were going to a seminary, which we did not believe in. It was as if you had lost your faith and were turning against us and God. We didn't know much about what was right or wrong with seminary, but we went along with it for a while. We thought, maybe, you didn't want to see us, that you had rejected us."

"I can understand that. They told me, too, not to contact anyone. I wish I hadn't listened. I was trying to help the group but shouldn't have paid any attention to them. But I was trying to be cooperative and trust the best for you guys. I always wanted the best for all of you, and I didn't understand everything as well, then, myself … It sounds as if we were had from both sides."

Both agreed. And then one said, "So a few weeks passed, and they began to make all sorts of weird accusations about you that don't fit you, that made you look bad. But we know now they were lying."

"What do you mean?"

"Well, they blamed it on your dad, that you had talked to your dad."

On the surface that made no sense. But because my father had attended some of the meetings with me, they had an outsider who they could blame for my actions. They couldn't accept that I had thought for myself, so someone must have put the idea in my head, and my dad made a convenient target.

The one continued. "Then they blamed it on other close friends of yours not in the church. Then they made accusations about you that we know are not true."

I didn't care to hear the details; it was typical stuff that gets brought up when one party wants to degrade another and holds no merit.

The guys told how they began to put two and two together, and then the leaders kicked someone else out, this time a woman. She had not been as faithful and devoted as they wanted people to be. So one Sunday morning, they proceeded to castigate her and expose her as a sinner and throw her out. They accused her of adultery, which

in the University of Santa Barbara, Goleta community is a laugher.
Sex was completely open in that place at that time, and this woman
had been involved in its openness. They had expelled her, though,
all in the name of purifying the church. She was not strong enough
to know what was happening, and it devastated her. She needed a
Christ person to come by as Jesus did for outcasts. But there was no
such person around for her.

In the cafeteria that afternoon, these two told me that they had
figured out I was not a bad guy at all and that Bill and Harry were
literally running the church by now and trying to run their families
and even dictate how the people should run their lives.

"Terry," they said, "we've come to say we are sorry and how
wrong we were. We should have been alert."

I can't recall too many times in my life when someone came
to apologize to me. It seemed quite strange, but the words sounded
like music.

Then they paused, said nothing. I hadn't responded for some
reason; I was so surprised, and then it became obvious they wanted
a response from me.

"Yes, of course," I said, and everyone felt better. It was a no-
brainer to me. But they wanted to know I respected them, accepted
them, and approved of their journey. They did want to know I accepted
their apology, but they also wanted me to verify their lives now as
they set out apart from the group.

"Some of the other people feel as we do, but some are scared."

That made me feel that more was behind their visit, that maybe
they were looking to me for help. It left me somewhat troubled, and
when I got back to my dad's room and told him the story, he gave
me some good advice.

"Just let it go. Accept their apology, but you have no need to
keep in touch."

So, I let it go. And I was glad some of the others were seeing
light. I had had no idea at the time I made my decision to go to seminary that the situation in the community had deteriorated to such

an extent. I had only had a gut instinct that things weren't right, and I'm glad I had listened.

After the visit with the two members, I had a tempting thought that I could hang around and help people, but my better mind said, no, I would probably continue to make some of the same mistakes others had, and my life's purpose was not destined for that kind of ministry.

I knew this part of my spiritual journey had run its course. I had gained a lot in the various twists and turns that I wouldn't trade for anything. I now knew some areas where not to go to get more of God in my life and develop spiritual enlightenment.

My path, though, did not end with seminary, but the appeal of a place like a seminary where we would study theology, church history, and the Bible all day seemed terribly exciting, especially to one so starved of such knowledge.

Going to seminary was one of the wisest choices I ever made, presenting me with a resting place—not for stopping but just to pass through—on my way to meeting my spiritual goal. It challenged me, gave me a new foundation, and provided a chance to deepen my faith. I had some fun times, and I would not trade the experience for the world. But what I learned there was truly tough to chew. The concepts were so foreign to my previous theological education I had trouble accepting them—so much that I was tempted to quit. But I didn't. Instead, I made the adjustments I needed to. And I stayed the course.

CHAPTER 13

Only the educated are free.

Epictetus
Greek philosopher, former slave

"Hi, I'm Terry Thomas," I announced with reserved excitement as I introduced myself in the seminary registrar's office just off the front hallway of Old Main in St. Paul, Minnesota. I had transported myself across country by now, had located the campus, and had found the stately, old brick building at Luther Seminary, the kind with high ceilings and glass transoms over the doors. To get to Old Main, I had sauntered over the crisscrossing walkways covered with the outstretched canopy of massive, full green hemlocks, which now in early summer, blossomed out at their peak. This was a super time to arrive.

"We've been looking for you, and we're glad you are here," the short, slender, red-haired young woman said from behind the high counter with spritely enthusiasm. With a hundred or so other students coming in, she was looking for *me*? True. As we entered the registrar's office for the first time, Carol made each new student feel as if he or she were the only person in the world that mattered at the moment. She knew what it was like for new students to roll in from across the country in whatever vehicle they could keep running to a new place with new people and embark on a new education. I found out later she actually did make it her practice in prayer to know every single new student on the list before he or she arrived. And to top that, before we arrived, she held up our photos, which we had submitted in our application, when she prayed for us, one at a time. There was a spiritually minded person. Some years later, I heard that Carol enrolled as a student and became a pastor herself, and I am sure she was a good one.

In my spirituality endeavors, I was having many lives in one: I had done evangelical work, written a book, and made efforts to create local, community churches. Now I looked forward to a seminary education and becoming a church pastor of a traditional church. I felt like Solomon in the Bible who said he had tried everything under the sun, and I was doing my best to pack a wealth of spiritual experience into my life.

Even then, I could agree with what Lou Holtz once said, "I am not what I want to be, I am not what I ought to be, I am not what I am going to be, but thank God, I am not what I used to be." I was learning as I progressed on my path, keeping what I needed philosophically and discarding what no longer served me. Similarly, the founder of Macy's, Rowland Hussey Macy, went bankrupt seven times, but he kept learning and kept trying before finding ultimate success in his retail business. Setbacks didn't deter him, and they didn't hold me back. My goal was not to make a material fortune, as good as that mission can be, but to find what worked in life in other areas. And here before me in seminary was a brand new chapter in life, actually, a brand new book I would be living. Everyone I had known for the past ten years was now behind me. The books were new. The geography was new. The people and their attitude about life were new. Even the smell of the old wood was new. It was summer, a new season—markedly different from the previous one—there in Minnesota, too, and I felt good.

I was embarking to learn in a formal setting. Playwright Wilson Mizner, quite an unusual character of many trades, wisely wrote, "I respect faith, but doubt is what gets you an education." I would get one fantastic education as I encountered many opportunities to doubt. Out of those doubts would be the beginnings of new life.

My new endeavor would force me to question many of my sacred beliefs, and while this was no easier for me than for most people, the process benefited me. Starting from the ground up would require redoing the foundation. We tossed everything aside, questioning each idea: Do we need this? Will it support us? Does it help? We discarded knowledge passed along through the generations that truly did not serve well. But, oh, we had constructed such a solid foundation over the years, poured deep in the religious instructions of our childhood, strengthened over time, that at first, it barely nudged as the wrecking ball of our questioning attacked it. Seminary was a tough place to study, and for good reason.

However, certain doctrines—like the one that had hit me so hard as a child, original sin, as well as the two natures of Christ, the Trinity, the Second Coming, all foundational in the Western church since the fourth century—were not challenged, even if reinterpreted. To be ordained, a student had to agree to them, as well as to the Lutheran Confessions. The doubts and challenges to faith rolled around inside those boxes.

More than once, I felt my stomach rumble with resistance as concepts from childhood Sunday school were questioned. It was not easy to get the head and heart working together. For example, to challenge an idea about God that came from my grandmother was like challenging the veracity of my grandmother herself. But I carried on, and we made it.

As I surveyed my new challenge that summer, I thought back to Santa Barbara six months earlier. I had run into one of the members on the street back then, and even though he wasn't supposed to be talking to me, he had asked, "Terry, why would you go to seminary? You already wrote a book on faith. Won't it be a waste of your life?"

"Yes," was my thought, and I understood the basis for his question. But I scanned the mess we had made of trying to do church without it over the past few years in Eugene and California, and I felt we were goofing up with no chance of hitting spiritual enlightenment on any of our tacks. Plus, we needed to appreciate and integrate more outside knowledge. Science was coming up with all sorts of information that made the Bible look silly if taken literally. Psychology was discovering aspects of human behavior that made other parts of the Bible obsolete. And history? Archaeology and other evidence were showing the Bible was not necessarily facts or history as we know it today but more an interpretation of events and stories to fit a particular purpose at the time. The Bible would always have a place in our lives, but not always defined the same way. Changing times would dictate a change in what we gained from it and how it helped us deal with life. Hundreds of years ago, its place, perhaps, was different than it was now and what it would be going forward in the world. I didn't have the tools to put it together in my mind as I do now, but I had the gut feeling something was missing. For me to begin looking at it in this new way was not easy on my emotions. But I ploughed ahead.

Back behind the counter in the registrar's office in Old Main that first day was also a young faculty member of Old Testament, whose teaching and demeanor I would grow to enjoy and definitely appreciate later, Dr. Dan Simondson. He, also, had something to do with registration. I believe he was the lead faculty member to study applications and recommend which students to accept or deny, and his presence seemed to give his stamp of approval to "his" arriving students. His genuine smile and the deep sincerity in his eyes cemented my feelings that I had arrived at the right place. My first day on the seminary grounds felt positive, and I felt welcomed and valued.

I also felt another presence supporting me in this new environment.

Before leaving for seminary, my dad died of cancer, and I had spent his last weeks close by him. In the mornings as he lay in bed, I would read something from the Bible for him and pray, and then I'd play around with my harmonica until he said it was getting on his nerves. We were reversing roles—father and son. By the end, his cancer was moving fast and so debilitating that I was almost carrying him to the bathroom. I learned to be nurse, too, and give intravenous shots. He loved my attending to him, and I loved being there and doing what I could. With my unfailing care for him, I think he felt totally, unconditionally loved from God.

Once he and I faced that he was dying, we had good talks about it.

My dad had always confided his deepest thoughts about life to me, starting as a kid, thoughts I knew he didn't share with anyone else, and I felt special. I looked up to him so much. I told him, "Dad, I don't know how I can live without your being here for me."

"You'll be okay," he said. He stared up at the ceiling and, with a sense of peace, said, "Now I know what my dad and father-in-law went through." His dad and my mother's dad had died years earlier. I began to realize something I still hold to, that when death is imminent, a peace and a jump-start in increased faith can flow as if from a hidden spring in the soul. I would see this in church members later, too, as sometimes I was the only one by their bedside when they left their bodies.

The grief was starting to pile up on me.

"I'm looking forward to getting going in seminary, Dad," I said later.

"You don't need it," he said without hesitation. "You already know what you are doing." That was one of the biggest compliments my dad ever paid to me, and I cherish it dearly. But it didn't help me with my ego and humility.

"You've got what it takes," he said, and this meant a lot because I don't think he had felt that way a few years earlier.

Just a few days before I left the West Coast for Minneapolis, Dad died, and we held his funeral to a packed church of four to five hundred. Although my dad never made a big name for himself, people liked him and respected him. Many, even pastors, came to him for advice, feeling free to share their troubles and knowing he would treat them gently. My grief was almost unbearable. I still miss my dad and even talk to him once in a while. I've had to get mad at him sometimes for things that come up in my mind, forgive him, love him, and accept him fully, and that has made a difference in my own life in accepting me as I am, too.

I can hear him saying, "Attaboy, you're doing it right; just keep on. Stick right in there."

For the next twenty years, I would learn much, but what I want to emphasize in this seminary chapter is the value I found in academic study along my spiritual pathway. But it could come only by making space for that new knowledge through the incredible emotional challenge and pain from releasing ideas planted in childhood and accepting new but better ones. Seminary for me was not as difficult as for some academically, and indeed, I loved the courses, the books, the lectures, every part. But the challenge for me was when I ran up against stark, hard walls of resistance in my own emotional experience and mind that I would need to deal with. I had to face up to and change some naïve beliefs I grew up with if I was to be a credible spiritual leader—not that I cared to be a leader of sorts, but I wanted to lead myself and not be a follower of unthinking religious people who are out of balance.

So I got settled in St. Paul and could hardly wait to start Greek that summer, really and truly, and to read the Bible in one of its original, ancient languages and try to get a more accurate reading of the Bible itself. Over the previous couple of years at my small desk in my bedroom in California, I had actually picked up a couple Bibles in Greek and an old Greek grammar book and done some figuring out on my own.

But it would not be all study. I stepped into Minnesota in the era when the Minnesota Vikings were at their peak and appeared in something like four Super Bowls over the span of a few years, even though they never won. Football was the biggest thing going in the fall, and the town went crazy. Mr. Unbelievable Scrambler himself, Fran Tarkenton, was the quarterback and one of the city's heroes, along with the feared four defensive linemen nicknamed "The Purple Eaters" (Page, Eller, Marshal, and Larsen), all coached by town favorite to this day, Bud Grant (who is somewhere in his eighties as I write). Grant came from the Iron Range, had starred in three sports for the hometown university's Golden Gophers, played basketball for the local Minnesota Lakers that became the Los Angeles Lakers, and played pro football for the Philadelphia team. And when his pro football contract was not to his liking in Philadelphia, he moved to Canada and won several titles there as coach-player.

What I noticed about Bud Grant is he reflected the kind of quiet, introverted but tough personality that the area is famous for. He never grimaced; he never smiled. He reminded me of my full Norwegian great-grandparents—always the same, even though they churned inside with efforts to avoid feeling the pain of life. They had that Nordic knack of showing neither the pain nor the pleasure.

Grant's football teams played into twenty below zero at times, all outdoors, and he never let the players have heaters on the sidelines. If they did have heaters, he said, then they would think about getting to a heater. Yet they played their hearts out for him. He represented the kind of hardiness Scandinavians are famous for—suffering is good for the soul, even to the point of emotional self-flagellation. But like the Norwegian Vikings of old in Scandinavia, the harder the better.

In this stoical culture over the next few years, I would work on my personal spiritual development.

And after summer and fall—unlike Santa Barbara, here there was a winter—I about froze, whether indoors or out. No matter what building I was in, modern or older, when the wind kicked up, it seemed to blow right through the walls and windows and raise the curtains. I got some quilted long underwear from Sears, and I'm not sure I took that extra layer off until spring. One morning, I stood before the thermometer to see it had dipped to thirty-five degrees below zero. But they never called off class.

I must say that seminary was truly one of the most wonderful times of my life. I could have easily been a student bum and studied my life away in school, as either a student, teacher, or professor. Later, for a while, I did become a professor, but I had other callings on my path and so continued on.

What happened to me in seminary, though, in terms of my spiritual search, is that I got more into my head and I left a part of my heart behind, if that makes any sense. The brightest pastors in churches tend to become seminary professors. By and large, they rely on their left brain, which is the unemotional, intellectual side, and they are often clumsy in serving with the heart. Naturally, students tend to imitate professors, so the spirituality area I was seeking I had to do on my own. I meditated in the mornings on Psalms in the Bible. I even memorized some of the psalms. I read C. S. Lewis and got great spiritual input from Russian authors I read on the side, Tolstoy and Dostoevsky.

Besides academic studies, we also did fieldwork. Unfortunately, the Lutheran church the seminary assigned me to in my neighborhood was boring and uninspired with a congregation of negative people, to say the least. More people showed up to the quarterly congregational meetings in the basement to complain about the pastor than showed up in church on Sundays. It was their history. I discovered the problem was that they had never caught on to the attractive grace of God that Martin Luther had taught. I saw that the few who took communion sat in the first two rows. Those in the back "weren't good enough" to take communion and were sinners. So there it was, a divided church of hypocritical, complaining saints, heads held high, in the front and inferior Christians, eyes mostly downcast, in the back.

As a seminarian, I had to preach once or twice during the year for practice. The pastor was very happy not to have to prepare a sermon, and I was wound up and about fit to be tied by then. I got up and blasted away on grace. I think I even described the parable Jesus told about the Pharisee in the front who was thankful he was not like the sinner in the back and the sinner in the back who beat his chest and said, "God be merciful to me, a sinner." And I know I pointed out how Jesus said the one in back was justified. The congregation got the obvious point; I had not yet developed the bad habit of subtlety.

When the time came to kneel at the altar to receive communion, everyone came. Those in back streamed up the aisles and didn't care what the righteous in the front thought. We had to stop serving communion while the organist played a hymn so the ladies' committee could refill glasses because they did not have enough prepared, only enough for the usual few. Some in the front looked just a little ticked off, though, that those in the back thought they could come up and just take communion. I was probably a bit strong in my youthful enthusiasm because I nearly compelled "sinners" to come up to Jesus.

About four months later, it was my turn again, and it didn't help my ego this time, either, to see the church more than double its usual attendance. The parking lot was overflowing, and some people even had to park their cars down the street. I talked about each of us receiving a gracious and loving God without needing the old Germanic idea of working hard for everything you get. And although I don't remember the exact words, I do know they loved the message, making them feel good in God's eyes. I think many of them had felt religiously oppressed, and I was giving them a message of freedom and of belonging. Of course, I needed the message as much as anyone, and that was always the case. Fortunately, the pastor, Jerry Bangert, was happy just in not having to preach or prepare, and my popularity did not offend or threaten his ego.

I would not trade the seminary academics and intellectual work for anything. I would see that some who have their heart set on spiritual excellence but without intellectual balance can fly off into a spiritual woo-woo land. It is hard enough to avoid in either case.—with or without formal education.

Seminary was careful to teach the Bible in its context. This historical method simply acknowledges that the world changes over time, and words, concepts, and ideas change within historical periods. To read the same exact words, concepts, and parables in the Bible from the first century can mean something entirely different only a few years later, not to mention twenty centuries later. Hence, I had to learn to read the Bible in a new way. In addition, just because the spiritual concepts connected with the people then does not mean they are of importance for us today. This is not easy to take for those steeped in the authority of the literal reading of the Bible as I was.

I noticed how meanings of words in *Webster's Dictionary* changed over only the past two hundred years; imagine the changes over three thousand years.

For one example, I had to learn to read the book of Matthew as if I was in Matthew's church two thousand years ago and not as if he was writing for me today. And then I had to figure out how to apply those ideas that made sense two thousand years ago into today's world. Why would he and he alone say that God desires mercy and not sacrifice? What was his point? Why would he say that the Pharisees were like whitewashed tombs? What was his point? How could I transfer that concept into my life?

I would have to do the same with John. Why would John, alone, attribute to Jesus psychic powers of mind-reading? Why would John teach so much on the Holy Spirit? And why did he make no mention of a second coming? Why would no other book but John's have Jesus say we are all gods? Why would John never use the word "gospel"? Why would John alone not acknowledge apostles? If Jesus was so important to John, why would he degrade the idea of a virgin birth by ignoring the concept?

If we were to know the Bible for today, we needed to read the Bible with intelligence, or we would never gain genuine, authentic, and lasting spirituality that integrated its useful points.

One very tough example for me, emotionally, was when seminary taught that there were two accounts of creation in the first book of the Bible. How could this be, I thought. Creation happened only once. I had always assumed there was one story, and each account showed a different side. But the teacher showed the clear contradictions and required we figure it out ourselves too. Even so, some of the students would not accept it. I, myself, had emotional upheaval. My grandmother had been my first Sunday school teacher, and I associated my childish ideas with my love for her and her love for me, which made it more difficult for me to pass through this to the next level. But given the clear facts, I could not distort them to suit old, hardened ideas. I maintained my integrity and resolved the contradiction.

But then I remembered how, as I grew into adulthood, she often confided in me about herself and the Bible. "Terry," Grandma said to me when I was in my young twenties, and I can still hear her crisp voice with a bit of Norwegian accent and see the scowl, "I read the Bible every day and don't know what I am reading." I realized she might have been thrilled to be there in class with me and learn how to read the Bible intelligently and with solid honesty that made it easier to make sense of the words and contradictions.

I recalled, also, how she told that walking down the street as a little girl in Lawrence, Washington, she saw her Norwegian grandmother sitting by her front window reading her Bible, and that impressed her. What no one thought about was how people fall into a trap of reading the Bible like a good duty, not to get to heaven because they believe they are already on their way to heaven but to be a better Christian. And when they have little or no Bible training or don't know what they are reading, they could be better served to read only a verse or two they can apply and just work on that for a while, instead of reading many pages every day just to make the preacher happy. I wonder, now, if her grandmother would have said the same thing to my grandmother: "I read the Bible, but I don't know what I am reading."

As our professors challenged us, we also sometimes challenged them. And they did not always take well to the questioning any more than we did. One time, one of my instructors was explaining how there could not have been whatever the number of Israelites the Bible says crossed the desert, around a half million, and I agreed. But his reasoning did not make it so. He had a valid point but also some weak ones, and they came from scholarship through the previous two hundred years. So I raised my hand, not objecting, but with an honest question about two of his points. But he took my question as an objection, and that triggered him into anger. I certainly had not intended that to happen and felt sorry for my part in the matter. Evidently, he was even sorrier because he apologized to me in front of the class the next day. He did not retract the point—and shouldn't have—but he sincerely regretted his anger. His apology was the talk of the seminary. And it meant a lot to me, that when a professor made a mistake in front of the class he was big enough to apologize publicly. This was certainly a new, more open world to me than the one I had seen develop in Santa Barbara.

What was especially difficult emotionally was when I learned that many of Paul's letters were not by Paul at all, and the evidence was clear. Would I follow my emotional heart or the better sense in my head? I had loved Paul so much and read every one of his letters so many times that I nearly had them down by memory, thinking they were by Paul. It was like saying to a four-year-old, "There is no Santa Claus." No little child likes being told that, especially if people they love have created the myth that Santa Claus is real. Yet I learned it was common in those days to write under the name of someone people admired and that some of his letters had been written later by another person. At first, I fought the facts in my mind, but over time, I was able to understand and accept the truth in my heart.

To everyone's credit, many of the professors had been through the same process I was going through, so they had compassion and understanding. But they had to stand by honest reading, not the myth reading we had grown up with in Sunday school. Adjusting my viewpoint based on these revelations continued to challenge me. To grow forth in spiritual life is not now nor ever has been a smooth, upward climb for me. I had to learn to do what Paul taught in his authentic letters—to give up childish beliefs to move into more mature beliefs.

Knowing firsthand the training pastors received in seminary, I expected them to convey their wisdom to members of their church. But some years later when I worked in the ministry, I learned with distress that some in the pews so strongly objected to hearing the truth that differed from what they had heard for years that pastors tended to go along with the crowd. They reverted to the old ways, did not bring up what they knew from their schooling, and never brought their churches up to date. So children were still getting the same inferior information.

Little by little, I realized that a fundamentalist approach had more loopholes than I had ever known before and left more questions unanswered than answered.

Even as I took things quite seriously, I had some fun, too, being recognized for the work I had been doing for a number of years in studying the Bible before I reached seminary. For example, one of the New Testament professors, a Norwegian by the name of Olaf Storaasli, who passed away in 2006, took me under his wing. He recognized both my knowledge of the Bible (although I was still growing in the academic understanding of it) and my process to relearn the way to read it. Whenever Dr. Storaasli had to miss class, he would turn the class over to me. That was an honor, and my classmates liked my doing it. If he could, he knew how to authenticate students of all stripes and integrate them into an experience that would be most effective for them, the seminary, and the church. Dr. Storaasli was a true pastor-professor, and experiences like the ones he provided to me made my learning process easier. I was actively participating in the knowledge and not just absorbing it as a student at a seat.

One of the most fascinating seminary experiences for me was to return to Israel and participate in archeology for a summer. Six of us from my seminary got scholarships and were assigned to dig in Caesarea, Israel, on the seacoast. On a practical level, we learned to measure things out, slowly dig with a trowel, and reconstruct what was there. But we received greater benefit on the more subjective level. Through our on site reconstruction of biblical-era buildings and cities, we connected more directly to the Bible. Our work allowed us to spread out our knowledge and experience, grasp history and anthropology better, and use our increased insights to be a better pastor and teacher later.

Before it seemed I had hardly begun, it was time for me to graduate from seminary. Everyone at that time looked forward to his or her assignment to start a ministry. I had had one year of internship with a pastor in Willmar, Minnesota, a most interesting small town smack in the middle of the state. Because there was a small church out of town that couldn't afford a pastor and they needed someone with a little more experience from seminary but not yet finished, they had placed me there. I worked under the supervision of the pastor of the huge church in town, was in the big church halftime, and worked in the country church the other half.

The congregation numbered only a few, and a neighboring pastor told me he thought the little country church would be clos-ing in about April and most of the members would be then joining his church. He told me, "So don't get them too stirred up, Terry. Just help them shut down."

And if you believe I did that, you have not been paying attention. His words seemed self-serving to me, that he wanted all those members to make his own church larger. I believed that the little church was there for a reason, and that the members probably loved their church. Never, in my ideal, did I visualize going into the ministry to shut down a church. I saw myself as a church builder, and I always like a challenge.

CHAPTER 14

Grant me, O Lord, to know what I ought to know, to love what I ought to love, to praise what delights Thee most, to value what is precious in Thy sight, to hate what is offensive to Thee. Do not suffer me to judge according to the sight of my eyes, nor to pass sentence according to the hearing of the ears of ignorant men; but to discern with a true judgement between things visible and spiritual, and above all, always to inquire what is the good pleasure of Thy will.

Thomas à Kempis
Medieval monk

"Good morning, Pastor."
"Pastor, can you explain …?"
"Enjoyed the sermon, Pastor."
"You're the best, Pastor."

Pastor. Pastor. Pastor. I got used to the title and the status, maybe too much at times. It is easy to get caught up in the title. It set me apart and gave me a new identity. I was now a professional Christian, so people thought. In the eyes of some, a pastor is not a regular human any longer. Not a space alien, either, but someone automatically closer to God than the rest of the human race. Experiencing others' elevation of me as a new pastor surprised me and sometimes even bothered me. I was still an ordinary person, but the people did not perceive me in that way, and how they perceived me affected how I saw myself sometimes. Back and forth it went. They viewed me one way, which contributed to how I now saw myself, which bounced back to them in how they perceived me, and each bounce made this supposedly new me bigger in everyone's eyes, including my own sometimes.

Are pastors more Christian, which means more of Christ-in-them, than other people? Or is everyone in the Christian world inhabited by the same Christ?

In this chapter, I want to lift everyone into the realm of God and debunk the idea that "religious" people are closer to God. I found that being a pastor or in the clergy or a bishop is a job and has nothing at all to do with spirituality. In terms of joining the presence of God in daily life, which leads into spiritual consciousness, the ministry, surprisingly, has no advantage, none at all. The idea of a people or class holier than another is destructive to life into genuine spirituality and actually anti-Christian; everyone has an equal opportunity for a deep connection with God. In fact, I think everyone has the same challenge and prospect to create that spiritual relationship with him. No one has limited possibilities for spiritual advancement. No one needs to attain "clergy hood" for a deep relationship with God. No one needs special education or training to reach God.

But with this opportunity comes responsibility. Each person must do the work to advance his or her spirituality, no matter the job or career path in this life. But when clergy are portrayed as closer to God—not by every church all the time, but often enough—the people easily sit back and depend upon the pastor to do their spiritual development for them. And that never works for them. Pastors easily fall into the same trap, as did I sometimes. They try to do the work for the people. Instead, every person needs a fulfilling experience of God. But if they look to the pastor to do that for them and the pastor tries to do it, both lose out. And both must fail. How can anyone, minister or otherwise, give a person an experience with God? It has to happen between God and that person. Anyone wedging in between will lessen the relationship. A minister can help the person get that spiritual connection, but he or she cannot make it for the person; the individual must take that step. When the pastor thinks he or she has worked for the people but not let them make the direct connection to God themselves, he or she will have unhappy people who will feel cheated in not getting the spiritual experience they yearn for.

Sometimes pastors, as well as bishops (pastors who rule over other pastors) and others in special religious roles, stand on an invisible pedestal and bask in the special attention that goes with the title. Using their position and title to put themselves above others betrays the ideal Jesus had for a common domain for all people as humans. Titles are for the work they do on earth, not personal exaltation. And when they do fall into this error, they leave themselves vulnerable to all sorts of projections and expectations unrelated to who they really are as human persons and the work they actually perform

It is my belief, in fact, that the pastor is to be leading the way by example and coaching people into the presence of God as a player-coach. I well know that it is a tough task because people in the churches do not always want coaching into the presence of God. Many do, of course, but others do not see the value—perhaps because of a lack of examples.

I can't tell you how many times my barber, Derek, said, "Terry, you're a pastor. Send a prayer up for me. The Big Guy hears you but not me."

I learned to say, though, "Derek, your prayers are as good as anyone's if they are honest and authentic. Cut the bull. I'll pray for you but not because mine get there sooner or are more effective."

For me to be a pastor required four years of a carefully monitored education at the post-college level and then a public ordination into the ministry, and I respect that. It was a big deal. The same church in Bellingham, Washington, where my father's funeral had been held four years earlier was packed. The choir sang, special musicians played, and my uncles read from the Bible. It stirred the very soul. But I must tell you the truth. When I walked out that day yoked with colored stoles my sisters and mother had made, symbolizing that I was now an official pastor, under my skin I was the same guy I had been when I had walked in without them.

I had received training to serve the people with good news, to teach the Bible, to counsel the sick and dying, to give church leadership. But as far as more of Christ inhabiting me, no, not at all because of ordination. I had grown in creating more room for Christ in my life, but that had nothing to do with being ordained. In fact, that evening after the ceremony, my Uncle Irv said, "Well, Terry is still Terry to me."

Some pastors don't feel that way, I realized once I was one of them. They think ordination somehow changes them, elevates them above the layperson. And plenty of people besides the ministers like that idea. After all, isn't it great to have a friend or relative closer to God, someone who has an in with the Big Guy upstairs?

In fact, I find it sometimes can be more difficult for pastors to achieve higher consciousness because they can have a perception they are already there. So why try? They are tempted to listen to the people and believe they do not have to take the same medicine they dish out. They can also too easily get caught up with churchy mundane work and forget their own need for growing in spirituality.

But there is nothing automatic—no job, no profession, no religious endeavor, nothing—that gives one person an advantage over another in reaching a higher level in his or her relationship with God. Seminary does not do it. Reading books does not do it. Knowing "about" God does not do it.

I've yet to reach the spiritual peak in every moment of my life; I'm still working on that. But I do offer what I have found—a path that works in getting there, side trips to avoid, and signposts to ease the way. Those at the highest reaches say that the higher we get into comfort with our spirit, the more opportunity we still see for advancement, and the exploration and spiritual development expands and explodes before us with infinite possibilities. And we become less egoistic and more and more humble about it. A sure sign that people are not there, they say, is when they believe they have all the right understanding of God and religion, reject any doubt of their faith, and are, consequently, no longer growing. Doubt is that fertilizer for the soul that promotes spiritual growth.

I have nothing but admiration for good, people-oriented, humble pastors—or even proud pastors whose pride is rightly placed, for that matter. Each has felt a spiritual call at some point and is in his or her own journey. This is not about putting pastors down in any way. But it is about elevating all people into finding their own way into the presence of God.

I ran across a special passage from Kahill Gibran that intrigued me because it reinforced the idea that everyone has an equal opportunity to achieve the highest in spiritual consciousness: "Your daily life is your religion," he said in his essay on religion.

Richard Foster, a Quaker, put the same idea this way: "The discovery of God lies in the daily and the ordinary, not in the spectacular and the heroic. If we cannot find God in the routines of home and shop, then we will not find Him at all."

Astounding. This opposes the medieval church idea that still rumbles through us in Protestant teachings—that one ascends closer to God through sacraments and becoming a church professional.

Those who have read about Martin Luther, the reformer of the sixteenth century, are familiar with this same concept. He broke ground by discovering an entirely new spiritual life path that broke with the teachings in the Middle Ages. He said that the career (whether religious or not) is simply a calling, or we would say a job, and people of faith serve God through their career. The church is merely a support base. The career of pastor is no more elevated towards God than the junker, as Luther put it. The Protestant churches have not always paid full attention to Luther on this point, sorry to say.

Spiritual giants agree with Luther. Ernest Holmes, founder of Religious Science, said something that cuts against many people's spiritual goals when they move into professional ministry. "It is not necessary to spend your entire time in prayer and meditation. Rather, seek to make your work a prayer, your believing an act, your living an art. It is then that the object of your faith will be made visible to you. It is then that you shall 'kiss the lips of your desire.'"

Jesus taught this, too.

Then I noticed a passage from another spiritual giant, Emmet Fox, who passed away in 1951. "You build your consciousness by the things you do all day long," he said. "It is by such things that we are judged. God does not judge us. We judge ourselves by the consciousness we build, because life is a state of consciousness."

Spiritual consciousness in the daily activity is what counts the most. And I stumbled upon that realization, the joy in incorporating spirituality into my everyday life, when I worked in construction in California, before seminary. During lunch breaks, I had powerful spiritual connections. I drove a VW camper to job sites each day, and when it came to our half hour for lunch, I ran to my vehicle, grabbed my lunch sack and prayer book or Bible or whatever I was using at the moment, and spent time in meditation, although we did not call it meditation at that time. I would read slowly and pray about what I was reading and integrate that into my daily concerns. I never had sweeter times, even later as a pastor, and yearned to have more.

So when I got into the ministry as pastor, I thought how wonderful it will be to have more free time to study the Bible and pray. Ha! I laugh now. How easy it is to let yourself be tangled up in church business, meetings, incidental phone calls, sorting out staff conflicts, and the minutiae that eats away at time and the spirit. In addition, the denomination itself can find reasons upon reasons to pull pastors away and into meaningless meetings, meaningless to me, at least. But pastors felt they were working when they did these things, and work can become a justification for existence, a kind of addiction I had to monitor. To have a spiritual life, I had to create spiritual development time for myself. Some of that also spilled over into the people as I found ways to work with them that helped in their own spiritual endeavors.

In addition to demands that eat away at time and energy, ministers find limitations with the doctrines and principles. The church is a religion, a fixed, doctrinal model. It has agreed-upon rules and beliefs to uphold. Some think of it as liberating, and it can let one feel safe, secure, and protected within its boundary. But I also think of the doctrinal structure as a six-sided box without windows or doors. In other words, it is a closed system, leaving little room for different beliefs, and for those now moving into the spiritual consciousness path, it feels suffocating, heavy with dead air. The pastor, I found out, is an employee to guard the doctrines to keep the people safe and to advise various committees who oversee facets of the church.

Spirituality, on the other hand, as opposed to religion, breaks that mold and authorizes moving forward into new arenas with God.

It seeks truth and knows that no one truth is the final destination. So it leaves room for questions and spiritual exploration. I had known this but had no idea what this really meant until I retired from the ministry to pursue spirituality on a broader basis. From my wide reading and interests, I was finding there can be new ways to begin a fresh understanding of the nature of God.

So, having completed my four years of seminary study, graduated, and become an ordained minister, I arrived at my assignment in Minnesota in the glorious month of June. The snow had melted in central Minnesota, and flowers were popping out. Wild asparagus was sprouting on the small church grounds and around the cemetery, and some of the members had been picking from that asparagus for years. In June, the idea was they could pick some asparagus, then go down to the lake and catch a few fish, and there was dinner. Presto. Pretty cool.

As I drove around the gravel roads in the rural area of my little church on my first day, I came across the president of the congregation, Clarion, whom I'd never met before. In his early sixties, he was out at his mailbox with a hammer and nails. In spite of my experiences that gave me reason to criticize mainstream, church ministry, I enjoyed meeting many of the people.

"Well," Clarion said, "they did it again."

Looking down a little and peering up to me over his glasses' rims, he showed the faintest bit of a Nordic smile underneath. I noted his beautiful Norwegian brogue, too, that I later found throughout the entire community. Eventually, I couldn't help but pick it up myself. Later, he would always refer to me as his boy, and that was a compliment.

"Some kids came by in the night and knocked down the mailbox. This is the third time this summer." Clarion went on speaking with a twinkle in his eye and without any sign of anger. He understood. Evidently, he had been somewhat of a prankster himself in his early days when he traveled the farmlands of the Midwest and performed in air shows. He had gotten one of those red bi-winged planes and looped every direction with the complete bag of tricks. For all his wild stunt flying, Clarion surprised me with his natural humility. Why was I surprised? I don't know, except I had broad—and obviously unfounded—generalizations from my California and Campus Crusade days about spiritual Christians. Faced with reality, I was about to see some of them fly away and let whole people replace the limiting ideas of that label.

This country church was one of the older styles in the Midwest—white, traditional, with a tall steeple, surrounded by a cemetery. Later, when the Vacation Bible School had over one hundred fifty kids, we would have to go out in the farmer's field across the fence to create a baseball diamond.

Although the neighboring pastor had quietly told me he wanted me to shut this church down, my meeting the people soon gave me other ideas. I began to feel an outstanding potential if things were done with gusto, and I could see these good people wanted to keep their church.

One couple I met, Clarence and Stella, one of our farm families—down to earth, full of common sense, good people—had little knowledge to feed into my mind concerning the value of a spiritual search from a lofty point of view but tons of spiritual experience from living close to the earth their entire lives. I mean talk about kindness, unconditional love, and daily joy. Clarence, a tall, broad man with thick and strong rough working-farmer hands that I would grow accustomed to see in the men in the area, had a warm yet shy smile.

Clarence and Stella had a farm about five miles up the road and loved the church, which was fully integrated into their lives. When times were good, they kept their old farm equipment up-to-date and repaired but didn't run out and buy new tractors and farm implements. As a result, whenever it got tough, they had no debts.

One day, Stella said, "Terry, do you like chickens?"

"Yes, sure."

"Well, Clarence will get an extra fifty baby chicks in the spring to run around the place, and you can come over and help us butcher along about Labor Day." So there they ran—my chickens—out around the barn and through the long grass, picking worms and bugs all through the summer. By fall, they were plump and ready for the freezer. Here was the most basic kind of spirituality we were trying to do in Oregon, the sharing with one another.

Last I heard, years later when I was gone, after Stella died, her sister, Hazel, married Clarence and took wonderful care of him in their older years. He needed someone, and she needed someone to value her.

Then I got to know Marvin and Verna. I can't tell you about everyone, but some of these salt-of-the earth people are especially worth recalling. Marvin always wore a big smile under his full head of brown hair and was already retired. They lived on the lake, and Verna had a soothing, soft voice to kill for. Down by the lake, Marvin had an old ice-fishing house he never used that he slid out over the ice to the middle of the lake around mid November for me. I was supposed to do some fishing in the winter, not work all the time, they said. Me? A Type A personality? I needed that advice. I don't know who was pastoring whom.

At about two every afternoon, Verna got home from working in the school system, and they had coffee and played cribbage. Their dining room wall behind the archway had hundreds of games marked in code of who had won each game, and it showed years of history. If I happened by in the afternoon, I'd find them at the cribbage board like two kids having fun and with their coffee. And of course, the pot had coffee for a visitor like me who happened by.

You might think I'm as old as Abraham Lincoln the way I tell of these "old days," but much to my surprise, I found the area behind in technology and conveniences from what I had been used to on the West Coast. Everything moved in slow motion compared to Minneapolis or any large city.

Yet the people had full and interesting lives. And—I never would have guessed before—they provided a good model for moving into the spiritually conscious life. I was learning something about faith and life. These were things I'd never find in books in a library. I thought of one of the Beatitudes: "Blessed are the poor in spirit, for theirs is the Kingdom of Heaven." Not "will be" in a salvation sense, but now, they are citizens of the genuine, higher kingdom.

More than technology had passed by the area. Some rights that people elsewhere in the country took for granted still hadn't established themselves here in the heart of the Midwest. But they needed to, and as a person central to their community, I felt my share of the inevitable turmoil. Some things are fun, and some things get political without asking for them. The local bank had eleven employees, three men and eight women, one of whom belonged to my church. The women had trained all the men and helped them work up through the ranks to leadership and officer positions, while the women remained tellers in lower-paying jobs. The established culture expected women to stay home and raise the children. They would not be given any raises or management positions.

I think this biased system had festered for years when the longest-running woman employee got the bright idea one day that it wasn't fair. She went to the president and asked for a promotion. Well, he wasn't too smart. "You are born and bred to stay home and raise kids, so the bank will never reward you for working outside the home," he said. Too bad he didn't know the truly ancient history of the human race.

This stupid remark led to a court suit that drew national attention. A culture war broke out, and it ended up being the first bank strike in the United States. The women picketed throughout the blizzards and cold of winter, down to seventy degrees below with the wind chill. The young woman who was a member of my church wasn't terribly fond of the strike; nevertheless, all the women were on strike, and they stuck together like sisters.

I supported my member, and I was surprised not one of the other seven women had a pastor who supported them. Can you imagine? The town was against them. The political leaders were against them. Even some women in the community were against them.

My support was not grandiose or flamboyant, but they knew I was behind them. The church people were afraid to say much publicly, but they were glad I helped the women. Something spoke deeper to the eternal hearts of the people, I felt, deeper than the traditions that had developed over the years.

Regardless of my position in the matter, the women without supportive churches still suffered. The experience of one in particular shows how churches can be the very enemy of the spiritual life the people want.

One of the women was from a fundamentalist, religious family. She had married one of the sons of the farm and was suffering from what the family was saying to her. Her parents-in-law and husband had even had their pastor visit to straighten her out. Then my member had her come to see me to receive some desperately needed support. But what she told me caught me off guard although I shouldn't have been so shocked—I was supposed to be prepared for anything. I learned that the other pastor had hammered on her as an authoritarian parent might do to a child and told her she was sinning gravely and, unless she repented, she would go to hell. He was saying that working at the bank, then striking and making a public scene was going to send her to hell. The sad thing was that she was so programmed from years of upbringing to believe her pastor, the one with the "close connection to God," the one who knows the rules, that she couldn't help but fear she would go to hell. The situation was affecting her physically, too—she looked gaunt and was losing weight because her false guilt was killing her from the inside. No wonder she needed to talk to me.

To attain higher consciousness, we have to cleanse our minds and consciences of guilt. This woman's church that should have concentrated on helping its members with that goal and get closer to God was, instead, heaping guilt upon her and doing its best to keep her from reaching it. She was sinning according to her pastor—sinning against her religion's tradition—but no one told her it was not sinning against any commandment or teaching of Jesus.

This was one of my first brushes with the destructive power of a fundamentalist kind of religious group agenda. Far from guiding its member to a higher spiritual level, this church was tearing her apart. Something inside this young woman was trying to obey the religious roles, but at the same time, something deeper was telling her it was false. She was caught in the middle of a dilemma. The guilt from the authority figure of her pastor was so powerful that I never felt as if I was much help to this woman.

I wish there had been a quick and easy answer for this young woman, but to break free of religious bonds requires a willingness to do so and let the Spirit within guide us. It takes probing, learning from mistakes, and time. The solution was right there for this woman, close by, ready for her word to go into action. But she was not ready, and neither I, my caring church member on strike with her, nor anyone else could repair her dilemma for her. Last I heard, she had left her home and was wandering around like a lost soul.

Movie actress Lee Grant came to town and filmed a documentary about the bank strike and used my church for some scenes. And the women appeared on the *Today Show* and *Donahue*, not that these ordinary mid-America women were comfortable with publicity. But they had withstood so many cold, stormy days by now that—what the heck—they could do anything.

Despite the problems caused by the strike, after the stressful years in California, I found serving in that country church's life a welcome change. The work came easy to me and made me feel I was in the right place for the moment, that it was an important step on my quest. I could see the results of my efforts, that they were making a positive difference in people's lives.

Almost from the start, I felt I made an impact. When I got there, they had maybe forty in church on a Sunday and sixty members. Most of the members were older and loved their church and didn't know what would happen to it now that membership had gotten so small. The potential to turn the situation around energized me. If we added eighty, that would triple attendance. As it turned out, we moved to one hundred twenty-five. After the debacles in Santa Barbara, it felt good to have some success. I realized all they needed was a little leadership. Leadership by committee never works for something like this. So I had some ideas, and we got busy and began to give the building and grounds some new touches, thinking we might begin to attract new members.

I think the neighboring pastor who had warned me against this sort of thing was not getting happier. But I never told the members what he had said to me, or they might have believed him.

They put in new carpet. They put new siding on the outside from an old fund that had been sitting around. They actually depleted their treasury to nothing, which I told them I thought was a good idea (I knew, if they closed, another church would be glad to help themselves to what was left). In the basement, they covered the ceiling joists that had been exposed for seventy years.

After about nine months, a few visitors began to come but quite cautiously at first. I had developed in self-confidence and worked hard at preaching practical messages. But a nice-looking church and the good word from the pulpit were not enough. We were also becoming a social group. We had fun together. We had babysitters and went sledding. And I did some outreach work. I went to farmers who had left the church years before and sat on a bale of hay in their barns while they repaired equipment. We talked, we got acquainted, and they started coming back to church. I went to businesses and met the men. I taught a class for the ladies. I did my part, and the members did theirs; we all worked together. And before long, we doubled and eventually tripled in size. We got up to about three hundred in membership and had our one hundred fifty in Vacation Bible School.

Our new members included young couples, and as they began to have babies, we all rejoiced. But church community involves care for all stages of life, death as well as birth and all in between. We had our funerals, and they gave me a few bombshell revelations. My first funeral in the church was not long after I began. The deceased, Agnes, had been a stalwart member of the church for decades, perhaps fifty years, a single woman, tall with gray hair, who drove a white Ford Falcon from the 1960s. She had taught Sunday school for years and had always picked up a carload of kids to bring with her. She was demanding and never took no for an answer.

I thought her faith was invincible. But what was really working inside her shows how vulnerable we all are to the control of false guilt in our lives. In the hospital, I found her lying with her eyes closed and repeating a Bible verse over and over. "There is therefore now no condemnation for those who are in Christ Jesus," she kept saying.

"What's wrong?" I asked.

It took some doing, but she let me know some old "friends" from a church that had more rules than grace had been visiting her and reminding her of what they said was a sin she had committed years and years ago. It turned out she had been married briefly in her youthful years and then divorced as a young woman. These friends were telling her she was guilty of sin because, in her generation, it was considered a sin to divorce. She had kept it secret for many years, but now, facing death, fear and guilt came over her. I had my hands full to keep speaking of grace—not grace based on all the work she had done in the church, but just the simple love and goodness of God. It was wonderful how she did respond, overcome the accusers, and enter into peace before dying.

Another funeral early on was for Kenny, who had grown up in the church but was an engineer for the railroad in Billings, Montana. I never met him, but I knew his mother and family, and this was his home church. He was a generous and friendly sort, and after work one morning, after a night shift, he stopped for breakfast at a local cafe. They said he met a couple guys there for the first time, and they left together, he in his pickup and they in whatever they were driving. It looked as if they were asking him where to find some good fishing. As a lover of fishing and hunting, he knew the good spots.

Later, his body was found hidden in some brush alongside the road, out a couple miles from town. He had been robbed of what little he had on him and murdered. His fishing gear was also missing. They caught the guys a few weeks later and convicted them of murder, thanks in part to Kenny's fishing gear—they were still using it.

But it was up to me to lead that funeral, a tough one. Then a pastor of another church in the area who knew Kenny's mother showed up just before the funeral. He caught up with me in the basement and said he had asked her if he could say "a few words" at the funeral and she had said she wanted him to speak.

It was a tricky sort of invitation on his part, and I was caught between two hard choices. On the one hand, although the service had been planned in detail, this man could be included at the last minute. On the other, something about his attitude did not feel right, but I couldn't identify it, not enough to explain to Kenny's mother. So would I be generous? I had the final say, and I decided that if there were pieces to pick up, I would have to be large enough to do the job. How could I argue against a mourning mother who was just blindsided?

This pastor got up and in a condescending tone began to announce to the packed house that maybe Kenny had had time to ask for forgiveness at the last minute, lying in the bushes before he died. The mother sat there and began to moan and groan out loud. The pastor said it again. "Maybe Kenny had time at the last second, with his last breath there beside the road, to get forgiveness of his sins and be saved. We don't know. He might be saved." She moaned some more in tears and fear so loudly in the quiet church it reverberated from front to back.

I couldn't believe my ears. I thought I had misunderstood him, but no, he said it again. That someone actually believed something like that was beyond my scope of understanding. I realized this man had a belief that you had to ask for forgiveness of sins at the last minute before you died or you would miss heaven and go to hell. If you didn't, and you had even one little sin that you have not confessed, it goes unforgiven, and you go to hell. What junk. And some of the people sitting there had been taught that as kids. It was easy to fall back into that fear, doubt, and condemnation. How would you know you hadn't missed one of your sins?

Unfortunately, I felt enough damage had occurred, and I didn't want to use this young man's funeral for enlightening the church members on the topic. That would have to wait for another day. Instead, I did my best after he spoke to affirm the loving grace of God. At least I got in the final word.

I was running into some really strange beliefs out there, and it gave me a lot to preach against and for. Some of the people held onto their guilt feelings, condemnations, and religious practices like a baby clings to its blanket. Once we get a belief system under our skin and into our soul, it is almost impossible to break free of it.

It was important for me never to become an old boring pastor, just putting in my time for retirement as I thought some of the pastors might be doing. I hadn't lost my passion for God or nurturing a deep relationship with him or helping others to do the same. But some of my own thoughts were more and more in contradiction to the way the church as a denomination was going, and I found aspects of the church as an organization getting in my way. It seemed we spent more time at conventions debating politics than seeking God through prayer and Scripture, and we were worshipping in a style more in tune with the Middle Ages than our current time.

As much as I treasured my years as a pastor, assisting people in their own relationship with God, the time felt right for me to move forward. With a twinge of grief, I gave up the title, "pastor." My ministry had allowed me to serve people and the good news as I knew it then. But I was finding it had deficiencies. I had no idea where I was going next for career, but I did know God was leading me away from ministry.

I thought of the Indiana Jones scene where Indy (Harrison Ford) has to cross a canyon with no bridge over the deep, deep abyss. But as he closes his eyes and, with faith, takes the first step, a formerly invisible bridge appears. And, so, for me …

CHAPTER 15

The important thing is not to stop questioning.
Albert Einstein

ccording to Karl Barth, great theologian of the last century, we are all theologians, all of us. To advance in our faith, we all need to study to one degree or another, and we all need to put our minds to work and question our faith to arrive at our best truth. And this can be difficult for any of us, because it can launch us way out of our comfortable zone of habits, moral ideals, values, opinions, and beliefs and into new territory. But if we want the beliefs that move us forward into true spiritual enlightenment, then we need to challenge our opinions, get them in the open, and put them under the microscope of logic. The truth will remain, and the chaff will blow away and make room for better and higher truth. So, as long as we seek the truth, we have nothing to fear.

However, seeing the beloved chaff wisp away in the wind can be painful. And if people are like me, it is easy to think, "Well, I've done that; I've challenged my beliefs and moved forward already." Probably true, but I also find the process never ends. Anyone—whether religious or non religious; Christian, Jew, Moslem, Buddhist, Taoist, or any religion; new age, born again, or old age; powerfully advanced or not started yet—must constantly examine his or her faith.

When I had the incredible experience in the hospital hallway, it had been a spiritual mountain top, to be sure, a Mount-of-Transfiguration kind of experience for me. But like the disciples of old who were told not to stay and camp with Christ, I felt I needed to move forth into new arenas—that the experience was a launch pad, not a destination.

From witnesses and scientific evidence, we now know a spiritual world swirls around us, through us, and in us in both our spiritual atmosphere and physical dimensions—not just the space of the spiritual. As those twin prongs of spirituality and physicality come increasingly closer together in our understanding of life, we approach our ideal of heaven on earth. Consciousness of the unity of invisible spirit and the physical, visible world is increasing exponentially. That we are spiritual beings having a physical experience is not a new idea, but the awareness is rising rapidly with multitudes. So even as a pastor, I set out to move ahead in knowledge, even if my choices took me beyond the confines of the teachings of the church.

Things needed to change in religion, I believed, and I wanted to do my best to get to the heart of it. Not that people were unhappy, but that seemed to be part of the problem. Happiness in ignorance is one step before a fall.

I had heard one seminary professor say if the church of the future is to be effective, it must deal with four historic people who changed recent history: Thomas Jefferson (democracy), Charles Darwin (evolution), Karl Marx (Communism), and Sigmund Freud (psychology). I will add a fifth, Albert Einstein (physics). In other words, these figures changed how the world perceives reality, and religion must effectively integrate modern insights from political science, philosophy, the human sciences, and the hard sciences if it is to be effective with the multitudes. I felt called to participate in these arenas more fully.

I realized that, because Christianity had been so big and powerful in the world at one time, it seemed to feel above the need to pay attention to modern discoveries. As a result, it was slipping in its relevancy. The church in modern times felt it could just coast by under the name of God and keep its antiquarian, authoritarian ways.

Independent thinkers over the centuries have supported this idea of questioning the old and adapting their own religious thinking to life around their modern times. For example, the democratic thinker, Thomas Jefferson, created his own version of the Bible, and it was a treat for me to get a copy and read it. He cut and pasted from the old Scriptures a new, more streamlined Bible, discarding what didn't fit for him. He did literally what we all do in our minds when we read the Bible, extracting and remembering only what has meaning in our lives.

At one time, Christianity simply banished or burned at the stake scientists and independent thinkers whose ideas went against religion's teachings. But now, in the more civilized world, it has been tending to ignore them. And in turn, the people have been tending to ignore the churches—at least the traditional ones.

I felt I needed to get underneath what we do and why we do things a certain way in religion. Why did religion hang onto two- to five-thousand-year-old concepts and practices, as if the older the better? Why not subscribe to the slogan, "The newer the better"? I figured even Jesus was trying to break an antique mold when he said that, although Moses, who had written over one thousand years before Jesus's lifetime, spoke a truth to his generation, much of his writing no longer applied. Jesus overstepped Moses and instructed his followers to do certain things in certain newer ways and not follow the teachings of Moses, even though biblical. Coming from a Christian world, I found this discovery absolutely astounding. And it added to my freedom to move forward towards spirituality and still appreciate the Bible. I thought, if Jesus revised laws that went back twelve hundred years, why couldn't we revise religious laws that go back two thousand years?

My questioning continued, but I wanted to do more than challenge. I like Henry Ford's comment, "Don't find fault; find a remedy." I was going forward for my own knowledge, but also, I was looking for a solution, a remedy, because I was committed to the idea that all people need to be in touch with their spirituality to be complete and happy. If I was going to contribute much in the bigger picture, I would need more advanced, formal studies.

All this led me to the decision to enroll in a PhD study program at Marquette University in Milwaukee, Wisconsin, under one of America's leading Martin Luther scholars, Dr. Kenneth Hagen. The school, named after Catholic, French explorer Jacques Marquette, sits in downtown Milwaukee, only a few blocks from the shores of Lake Michigan. Milwaukee tends to have the same winds and weather of Chicago not far to the south—hot and humid in the summer and cold and snowy in the winter. The city has real seasons, and the weather goes to extremes—the worst snowstorm I ever experienced hit me in Milwaukee

Like most of us who set out on a course of study, I thought I was going to reinforce what I already believed and add to it. But to advance, I might have remembered, I would have to put myself through some rigorous questioning, which would cause me to leave some baggage behind, beliefs I didn't know I had. But the new knowledge I would gain would serve me for the rest of my life in my search for higher truth.

I had many courses to take first because a PhD in theology at Marquette required high proficiency in three general areas, not just one: Bible, theology, and church history. This intense academic study, on top of what I had acquired in seminary, left no room for fly-by-night thoughts and provided the solid foundation for the ideas I kept arriving at.

I had to pass reading proficiency examinations in German and French because my thesis research required I be comfortable in major theological languages in history, and it was assumed I already knew Greek and Latin. I could work also with Hebrew, if necessary, which I did need to a small degree. I even went to Germany one summer and studied German at the Goethe Institute. I loved this work, but I'm not a linguist, and learning languages came with a struggle. Thankfully, I didn't have to speak them all—just read them.

I took advanced courses for a few years, and then I went into a year of independent study, preparing for a general examination for two days before a faculty committee by writing answers to their questions in a closed and locked room all day and then defending my answers orally the next day to prove I knew the material. Only then was I allowed to go forward to build my PhD thesis.

The crowning accomplishment for any PhD candidate is the thesis—writing that breaks new ground, based upon solid research, and is usually published as an academic book. And I would have to defend my thesis before a faculty board at an open meeting, which other graduate students attended, as well as family and other friends.

"Terry, what are you thinking of for your thesis?" Professor Hagen asked me one summer day. It was getting close to decision time for my research subject and thesis, and my choice would prove to be one of the most significant decisions of my life.

"I'm not sure, really, Dr. Hagen," I said, as we sat in his small campus office.

"Terry, there is something in Luther that has never been fully discussed that I think you could take on," he began.

"I'm interested," I said.

"It is controversial. And tough. Luther said something two or three times that has puzzled scholars throughout all the centuries. No other Reformation leader said anything like it, and no one since has either. Conservatives of the centuries keep it quiet. Liberals don't know what to make of it."

"Well, there is nothing I love more than a good challenge," I said. "You've seen that in me over these years." Dr. Hagen knew his PhD candidates well; he treated us like colleagues and friends, and we were always welcome in his office. If he wasn't in, we had a key and could even sit behind his desk to do our work. "Okay," I continued, "so what do you have in mind?"

"There is a phrase in Luther that we are not sure how to handle: 'Christ against Scripture,' or in official Latin, *Christum contra Scripturam*. Why don't you research it and make that your doctoral thesis?"

It made sense, and I was eager to get going.

By this time, I had already been to both what were West Germany and East Germany at the time to do onsite studies, visiting primary locations of Luther's life and work. One unique opportunity for me that expands in my memory was in the Wartburg Castle on top of a mountain near Eisenach, like a jewel in a setting, where Luther was in hiding when he was a political outlaw and religiously banned from the church. Anyone who would steal his property or kill him would receive honor from Charles V, the Emperor of the Holy Roman Empire at the time. But Luther's popularity throughout Germany protected him, and he was never arrested or executed. I stopped in the little room with its small window overlooking the lush forests and valleys below and lingered at the small desk where Luther had translated the New Testament into German from Greek, which came to be known as the Luther Bible.

But what did I discover about his long ordeal of several years? For his time, Luther had a unique way of forming an intimate relationship with God, and this carried over into how he prayed. The late Heiko Oberman, dean of Luther studies worldwide over the last half-century, wrote, "In the later Middle Ages, scholastic theology and ... mysticism went their separate ways. But it is a unique characteristic of the theology of Luther that these two are reconciled and organically interwoven." Most people are either intellectual or mystical, but Luther was both which made him a rare genius.

One time, as an example of Luther's mystical side, a colleague of his walked by his tower office in Wittenberg (still right there—I saw it) and overheard Luther talking. At first, he thought Luther was having a heated conversation with another person in the room. But, no, he was praying—but not in the approved way. Most prayers at that time were read from prayer books to avoid saying a wrong word in prayer.

Luther's independent approach to religious matters encouraged me to move more and more into the spiritual tradition that developed in America in the eighteenth and nineteenth centuries, seen in the contributions of philosophical intellectual and spiritual leaders like Ralph Waldo Emerson and his friend Henry David Thoreau.

I also discovered how Luther advanced the common understanding of the gospel for his own age, and his example gave me the feeling I could do the same in my time. With all due respect for Luther, I could not accept all that he maintained, but I could accept his methods. He followed his own conscience as he interpreted

Scripture, translating his Bible to the end, always adding, subtracting, or substituting words. But for me to follow Luther's example, I would follow Scripture according to my own mind, not necessarily Luther's. Luther believed his ideas would last forever and needed no new theological ideas to express them. But our worldview is completely upside down to his world, or right side up, depending upon how we want to explain it. We needed spiritual guidance to match.

Luther had gone back to Paul's ideas expressed in Paul's language in Paul's time, and found his gospel in Paul. Two thousand years of philosophy and science after Paul, I felt I had to move forward and find a new way to find the nub and heart of the good news. Luther believed, as do many of us, that our understanding of the gospel is the right one and the only one and has always been the same. But through history, concepts and interpretations of terminology change, and even today, there are many different viewpoints.

Luther, then, became a pass-through arrow for me and not a stop sign, an inspiration and not the answer.

My third discovery, and the most important, concerned the Bible. I had read the Bible daily since I was eighteen years old; I loved it, and I knew it fairly well.

Luther's example of revising the idea of the gospel for his day released me from living under ancient, antique concepts and lifted me with the Bible as my background into the twentieth and twenty-first centuries. Luther did this by opening the doorway into a world of Biblical scholarship that followed over the next five hundred years. He became a forerunner to the development of the historical-critical method of Bible study because he employed the most current tools of his day to aid his studies—first, the Greek language resurrected by Erasmus and the Renaissance and, second, the printing press. For us, the tools of modern science and scientific methods to study literature help us interpret the Bible in a new light.

Dr. Hagen's suggestion for me to research the subject of Christ against Scripture was a godsend and led me to expansion in solid, well-thought-out spirituality.

Up until the sixteenth century, the final content of the book called the Bible was somewhat open and not officially decided upon. It was still a library of separate books and writings. Until Gutenberg invented the printing press in 1452, no Bible had been printed. And when he did print the first Bible, he gathered together Scriptures as they understood them and printed them in one big volume, one big book, called the Bible. Some books in the library were more important than others, and some were less important. But reading the individual books and, thus, recognizing their separateness—in being written by different people over vastly different time periods for very different reasons—would be more difficult to do now that all were in one bound volume.

Still, there was no "official" Bible until after 1547, a year after Luther's death, and yet Christian faith communities to this day have different books in their "sacred" Bibles.

My family was no different in this respect. Before my maternal grandfather died in Soap Lake, Washington, he called me to his bedside in the back of their apartment and said he was giving me a Bible. He called my grandmother in to get it, and I saw her reach through the sheer curtains high in the closet to retrieve it from its wrapping in tissue paper. It was a Luther Bible in German from 1776 that had been passed along down through the Supplee/Toler family. Grandpa took it, talked a little about it to me, but not much, and said it was mine. I would read it, value it, understand it, and I would know what to do with it. I still have it, a very heavy book on ancient, thick paper, bound in horsehide leather. This Luther Bible carried a holy significance to our family, as if it was more sacred than any other Bible, and now I was the torch bearer. But in reality, it was no more sacred. It is a piece from history and extremely meaningful to me and my family in that way, but as far as an accurate account of what Jesus said and did and a guide to spiritual enlightenment, it had no advantage over many other versions.

In my studies, I was finding myths both in and outside the Bible that needed to be set aside if I was to find truth in spirituality. Old beliefs were important to identify and set free. For example, over the last two hundred years and especially over the last seventy, through archaeology and literary studies, we have discovered books about Jesus that are older than the ones in the actual Bible.

As professor of Bible at the University of Wittenberg and recognized as the theological leader in Germany, Luther made his own decisions about the importance of each of the biblical writings. He separated the books into three groups, according to the value he saw in each, from most valuable to least. By letting Luther be a theological model for me, I would be able to sift through the Bible myself with an open mind and without laying equal claim to the authority of every book, page, and verse. If I had not done this, I could have been so fixated literally on the Bible that I might have been blocked from the wonderful presence of God in the Spirit, the higher spiritual consciousness. For me, the Bible would be a tool to get into higher consciousness—with eyes wide open and discerning. It is God first, not the Bible.

I am not bashing the Bible; nor did Luther. He, of all people, held it higher than, perhaps, anyone in his generation. But he found it had its place, and its place was not first. Jesus never said, "Love the Bible with all your heart, with all your mind, with all your soul, and with all your strength." He also never said, "Love your doctrines with all your heart, with all your mind, with all your soul, and with all your strength." He placed love of God and love of one another above all else.

As I worked through the research on my thesis, I also learned the background of Luther's Christ against Scripture statement. Once the Reformation was spreading, some fringe groups started teaching the people to keep all the laws of the Bible, and they were known as Sabbatarians. For instance, they claimed that they had to go to church on Saturday, and they quoted certain Bible passages to support their views. Luther said they could have the Bible; he would take Christ. That is the crux of it. In other words, these people were living under old laws, called an old testament or covenant. The Bible is only the queen, Luther taught, and not everything in it applies to us. The gospel, Christ, is the king. The term "Christ" in Christ against Scripture refers to more than Jesus Christ; it also includes the new covenant work of God, the gospel. It is larger than Jesus.

Luther did openly what Thomas Jefferson and most Bible readers do naturally but without realizing it. He selected parts of the Bible—which he called the Gospel, and that was valuable to him. He said the cultural laws of Moses were for those people at that time and had nothing to do with Luther and the Germans of his day. It was also true for Jesus, Luther taught. The Sermon on the Mount includes cultural laws for Luther that do not apply to us. That made me feel good because as I had been studying those laws for years, I had thought, how in the world could we enforce such things. We have advanced, and those admonishments no longer applied.

When I first encountered the real Martin Luther in the Westmont Library some ten years before, I never expected him to exert such influence over me. But he became a hero of mine as I learned more about him. And now, with Luther's help, I was gaining the ability to jump over barriers that kept me in a literalism and out of spirituality. It was time to get out of the confines of the antique store and into the fresh air and light.

You take the Scripture, Luther wrote in so many words, and I will take Christ, my gospel, my good news from the same Scriptures. And cultural laws, religious laws, or anything of that nature is not the good news but a step back into rigidity and powerlessness.

My Martin Luther studies did many things for me, but especially, they fed into my journey toward spiritual consciousness in several ways.

First, Luther's methods gave me the example to perform absolute excellence in scholarship, accepting the findings no matter where they led, and at the same time to have a mystical experience of God. In other words, I could pursue my spiritual journey with honest integrity intellectually, as well as spiritually. Second, he advanced the gospel in his own time, and in so doing, he gave freedom for the next generations to advance the gospel for themselves. Just as Jesus updated Moses's gospel from well over a thousand years before, I, too, can update it for me. Third, Luther opened the doorway to move through and perhaps even around Scripture to get to God.

And Martin Luther's door opened to everyone without reserve. He said, "All who call on God in true faith, earnestly from the heart, will certainly be heard, and will receive what they have asked and desired." As I ponder the true heart of Martin Luther, I do not believe we are really that far apart; like me, he loved God and sought truth.

CHAPTER 16

The one unchangeable certainty is that nothing is certain or unchangeable.

John F. Kennedy

"Hey, Terry," a young friend said to me a few years later as I was puttering around in my kitchen, preparing a meal. "Here're the tapes the guys loaned me. They're really excited about 'em."

Life had taken some disappointing turns, but I had put them and their sadness behind me. I was happily moving forward and finding, as I usually did, that downturns often opened up the soil of my heart for new life to take root and spring up. In other words, I was ready for another step in my spiritual search.

"They're motivational," my friend said as our conversation in the kitchen continued. Just out of high school, he was doing direct sales for Cutco Knives. He had practiced his pitch on me, and I loved his honest, humble style. It reminded me of my first summer job out of high school, selling *Collier Encyclopedia* door-to-door in Seattle. But he was not selling the tapes, just excited about them—his sales organization was asking the guys to listen to them, and he thought they might interest me.

"Can I see the tapes?" I asked, more because I knew he wanted me to than out of any desire to listen to them. Truth be known, motivational tapes and speakers were far from my interest.

"I borrowed them, but if you want a copy, you'll have to buy a set."

The only tape sets I had ever bought were intellectual, like the history of the Enlightenment or "Why Herodotus is a Leading Historian." But these tapes, according to my friend, were fresh cut and by a young up-and-coming pop psychologist/speaker, Tony Robbins. I'd never heard of him. Nor did I have any interest in his type of motivational help. My academic background had told me little of such people. Sure, many in the general public were embracing his kind, listening and learning from their messages, making Robbins and others popular, giving the "pop" to their title, but I knew better.

Academia had dismissed pop psychology, and I had agreed—based not on any analysis but merely on its bias. But as Luther showed in his approach to the study of the Bible, we need to keep our mind open, questioning, and logically analytical. Luther, himself, wrote countless "pop" tracts which the new printing presses allowed him to publish, ones popular among the masses in his time, and his example served to help me open my mind beyond the academic biases

I realized with dismay that I had a full, traditional education at the highest level but had been sheltered from the newest developments on the cutting edge of American ideas. And the bias that had kept that and other knowledge from me still shelters many of us from new information that can truly heal us and move us forward, material both readily available to us and potentially beneficial.

By this time, I wanted a full education, beyond the formal classroom, and I was dismayed this area had been sheltered from my awareness. I was willing and eager to explore, and this young man's suggestion piqued my interest.

So I bought the tapes and listened to them many times through. Tony Robbins was my introduction to an entire library of writers and speakers that would occupy my inquisitive mind for the next few years and later lead me into an entirely new world of spiritual awareness. I have never left my appreciation of these men and women in this field; they added a fresh step in my journey towards a fuller spiritual awareness. As my heart opened to these new philosophers/psychologists and as I began to see incredible value coming through them, I also could see their ideas were violating traditional church teaching. In other words, even though they brought value to people, they seemed to be teaching heresy. Then my mind went back to one afternoon, about four years before, when I was sitting outdoors in the spring sunshine with another pastor in my town.

Mike, a tall, dark-haired man with bold rimmed glasses, in vogue at the time, always came across as laid back and easy going. We were planning a joint sunrise Easter service. By this time, as well as a pastor, I was also an adjunct professor of theology at Marquette University.

He proposed some ideas that I resisted.

"Mike," I said, "you know, of course, the church decided long ago that certain doctrines were the right ones." I had become rather expert in the development of church doctrine in my doctoral thesis and in studying Luther over the previous years. Luther would never have opened the door to reconsidering these "official" doctrines that Mike was advocating. I went on to list some early church heresies—doctrines the official church had rejected years and years ago when it had moved from a localized church of Palestine into the greater world of Rome. Mike listened intently.

"I think I am doing just about all of those things," he said thoughtfully.

"You mean you might be more of a heretic?"

"If you put it that way—because I accept the things you said the church was against at that time—then that makes me a heretic to them in their estimation."

We sat quietly out or doors. I was literally shocked. But I respected the man—he was smart, had the respect of good people, and did wonderful pastoral care for his members. I felt a contradiction. How could one of the best pastors I knew have such a wide definition of faith? How could he hold to heresy? But was it heresy for us now or more what they determined was heresy for them at their time? I did not know what to say. After a few minutes, we moved on in our discussion.

My giving Mike the label of "heretic" didn't faze him at all, and he showed no arrogance. In other words, it did not threaten him to think he was a heretic according to fourth-century definitions. For him, it was like looking at an antique and saying, "Well, I'd rather have modern furniture."

I let the issue go. But it stuck in my mind and rested there, waiting to be brought to the surface at the right time. I believe God was planting more seeds in me in answer to my prayers for clarity in my spiritual seeking. That conversation with Mike would pop into my mind from time to time, and when the Tony Robbins tapes idea came up, the seed began sprouting. For me, Tony Robbins would seem like a theological heretic—but would I change my view of heresy and not merely follow party line?

Over the years, I began to realize that the ones called heretics were the ones who usually did their own thinking and came up with their own conclusions, not necessarily the conclusions handed to them by the church councils and conventions. These heretics voted with their own conscience, no matter what it cost them personally, and it often did cost dearly.

At the same time, while I put all my faith in God to help me with everything, I was realizing that my own theology was not able to save me in a practical way. I began to feel if a belief system was valid, it had to work in practical, daily life for the people. If it was just about escaping hell and going to heaven, no thanks for me anymore. I was coming to the point that I wanted what worked here and now—what helped bridge the ideal of heaven from the afterlife to this life now.

Ultimately, it occurred to me that many of the teachers in the motivational, self-help work were doing more gospel work (good news work) than much of the church was doing. Shocking statement, I know, but let's explore that.

If the church's gospel is from Jesus, then he is the model for how to put his message into action, not a model to keep repeating his words. His words applied to his time in history for the people in that world and with that worldview; and they might not have relevance today. So I took a fresh look at my beliefs in light of what I had learned through the Tony Robbins tapes and books I was reading. I noticed the tapes didn't say much about God, but then, I realized that Jesus, also, didn't teach as much about God as about human beings and how to get along with each other. What Jesus said rang the bells of his generation because the multitudes came in record numbers and hung on every word. Jesus spoke to the people's emotional, experiential, and sensual needs. The little theology he taught tended towards trusting in a father who would care for them. It was this domain, which is called the Kingdom of God, that he was trying to create with the people.

My theological education gave me better knowledge in classical theology—its origins and purposes—but it stopped short in giving me faith. And by faith, I mean that which adds self-confidence over fear and worry, is based in someone greater than I am, and I connect with consistently and trustingly. And, of course, it could not because faith is a process, something we have to go through ourselves. Someone can't hand faith to us, any more than the propositions of classical theology can make it true for us. Faith is out, moving through rapids of life with trust in a kind heavenly father. When we come into situations that challenge us, real, hard-life problems, we either find our faith or realize we lack it. Real faith must operate in such ongoing activity, mental and physical, and not rest on the past and sink into death. Even though a theological point was life at one time, it must forge forward constantly into new life. Each faith step for me was landing on a new steppingstone across a stream, and to stop and try living on a steppingstone is certain death. The stone is there to walk across, not to live on forever.

Many religions make a mistake at this point. Too often, they make themselves the spiritual destination and hold us back from our forward thrust into independent spiritual life. And we let them do this. But for spiritually alert people who truly want enlightenment, they begin to treat their religion for what it is, and sometimes they even have to break away from it to be free.

So, too for me. My taking the next step was not easy, especially when it involved moving from what my background called immutable law. Yet, I realized the very idea of heresy was a limiting idea, limiting faith. Jesus, himself, was a heretic in his day because his work, according to the religious authorities, was out of bounds, and for that he was crucified. As I mentioned earlier, Paul said faith was a process of "faith unto faith," which means faith at one level leads to a greater faith at a higher level. Each level builds upon the previous, increasing in strength, in this always-expanding process.

As I read the pop psychologists and heard the motivational speakers, I found incredible faith in all of these teachers, no matter their particular religion—which puzzled me at first. They did not all have the same name for it, and some did not even mention God. But, like Jesus, they talked to the people about the people. They gave guidance on how to have positive relationships with others, how to have a happier life, how to live in integrity. And they based their advice on faith—in ourselves and in the ability of God to work with us to make happen what we wanted. As Jesus said, "With God, all things are possible."

Over the next few months and years, I read authors like Napoleon Hill, who taught a self-development process that touched people's emotional and intellectual lives. *As a Man Thinketh, Think and Grow Rich,* and *The Power of Positive Thinking* became favorites I read over and over. Later, I added Steven Covey, Brian Tracey, and Wayne Dyer, a favorite, both for his content and easy reading style.

I discovered, on the one hand, the self-help movement that guided people in their quest for a happy, balanced, passionate life, often with spiritual fulfillment as well, but I saw, on the other, the churches not only failing to provide the same to their members but even fostering conditions that prevented people from finding what they needed. By focusing on sin, religions gave people more reasons to worry and fear and not the ability to overcome it. Where was the faith in that? Those who worry and yet claim to have faith really have no faith at all.

But the self-development movement gave people effective rules to overcome the destruction of worry in their lives. The doctrines of the church were not practical enough to accomplish this. What they taught came close to what I found, for example, in Norman Vincent Peale's *The Power of Positive Thinking.* Dr. Peale was a pastor but out of the normal boundaries of traditional orthodox religion. When I saw that Napoleon Hill used his faith to heal his son of deafness, I was thoroughly stunned. How could this be? He was not orthodox in his faith. My dilemma came closer and closer to a head. I would need to expand my idea of faith and become more inclusive in who were God's people if I was to be honest about the facts of human life. And with my spiritual quest always in my mind, I saw I needed to go from the faith I had formed in my upbringing and my religious training to the new and next level of faith I would be finding through leaders in this movement.

Unfortunately, my academic training had set some barriers in the way to my benefiting from those in the self-help movement. The teachers and professors, who had such strong influence on the thinking in the church, dismissed this body of knowledge lightly and yet had never picked up one of the books or read them, as far as I could ever tell. They did to us what was done to them by their professors, and their influence to an entire generation of new pastors was beyond belief. Even if these folks outside normal church ranks were enemies of orthodox doctrine, they deserved better than degradation in the seminary classrooms. But then, heretics in the early church got no love either.

One preacher in particular received an especially scathing treatment when I was in seminary, poisoning my mind about him as well as others in the motivational/self-development movement. And although this incident involves one preacher, the beliefs behind it applied in general to those not on the "church approved" list. This example shows how tough it can be for Christian people to keep following a living God into higher levels of greatness, especially when the path goes against the traditional doctrines they have been taught.

While taking summer classes in the seminary, a student across the classroom from me in the elective course, Great Theologians, raised his hand and asked the professor a question about Paul Tillich, one of the two greatest theologians of the last century. I have forgotten the professor's name, but he came from a Swedish Lutheran background and spoke with a loud, deep, raspy voice, an authoritarian voice. He saw himself in the tradition of great European theologians of the past who held themselves above the students and the affairs of everyday concerns. Any stance other than aloofness would have been considered a weakness.

The question from the student was, "Dr. _____, is Paul Tillich's thought something like the thought of Robert Schuller?"

Robert Schuller, founder of the Crystal Cathedral in Garden Grove, California, a couple miles from Disneyland, started a drive-in church in the 1950s that later led to his famous *Hour of Power* television church program. He taught practical living and had a huge following, and his ministry grew into a worldwide influence, including even the Soviet Union and Moslem countries.

The student had asked his question in all sincerity, but he had failed to understand the church's stance on preachers outside the mainstream, such as Schuller. He would soon learn. I was sitting in the back right, near the door. I can still see the setting as clear as can be and hear the quick retort.

"I DIDN'T KNOW ROBERT SCHULLER THOUGHT," he belted out. And the classroom broke into hilarious laughter.

A highly charged episode like that from a well-regarded professor and infused with intense emotion (laughter, in this case) can stick in the back of students' minds and color their opinions for life, for good or for ill. This professor's response certainly stayed with me, and until I knew better, for ill. Such a grip on the mind took tremendous power to break, as I did a few years later when I faced the works of motivational/inspirational writers and those, including Robert Schuller, aligned with them.

And we students in the seminary classroom would influence thousands because we were preachers in training. When a respected professor makes a dramatic, opinionated statement with the force of fact, it moves into the subconsciousness of the students' minds. The only way to get one's own independent, thought-out opinion up and running is to go out in the world, get some personal experience, and then reflect hard and openly upon it. Otherwise, we are operating like most of the world, which is in ignorance and with knee-jerk reaction to past programming. Helping others break free of religious, mind-gripping control at the subconscious level by showing how I did it is one of the main purposes in this book.

I do not like to be told I am programmed and neither does anyone else. But one conversation with a marketing professional, and we will see how programmed we truly are. And marketers like it when we deny it and think we are independent thinkers because they know, of all people, we who swear off the influence are the ones most vulnerable to programming because we are blind to it.

That classroom episode settled any positive consideration I might have had of Robert Schuller and turned him negative in my mind. Even though the respected former Vice President Hubert Humphrey of Minnesota requested before his death that Robert Schuller come to Minnesota to perform his funeral, I remained steadfast in my negative opinion of the man.

The story gets more intriguing. Move the calendar ahead a few years where I now have a subconscious negative feeling towards Robert Schuller, or anyone like him. The stage is set. I was aware that Robert Schuller had a long-running TV church service program on Sunday mornings. When I visited older, home-bound parishioners who could not come to church, some mentioned they enjoyed TV church at home, thinking I would be happy they were getting some church service. And the pastor they got the most from? Robert Schuller. This did not set well with me because I did not feel they were getting a good gospel. They were accepting practical help in daily life from an alternative religious source, and I, like many religious leaders, was programmed towards exclusive, orthodox theology.

And the programming remained with a firm foothold. Now, a middle-aged couple, she with strikingly blond hair and he with distinguished gray, faithful in my congregation, salt-of-the-earth people everyone liked, were ushering one Sunday morning, and the woman made a comment to me as they were folding bulletins.

"Pastor," she said, "we are so happy to be here every Sunday and thankful to have our church. And we got up as we always do every Sunday and started with Dr. Schuller, and now we've come to our church. He really gets us going before we get here."

"Humph." What was I to think?

They believed that Pastor Robert Schuller and I were giving the same message for them in different ways. And she meant her statement as a compliment, putting me on the same level as the internationally known Dr. Schuller. But I did not take it as a compliment.

It would be like saying to your doctor, "Hey, doc, I got my herbs from the guy with the shop down the street before I came over to see you today, and I feel better. I thought you'd be happy to hear that."

I am glad, though; my heart was open enough to overcome the subconscious thoughts planted by the seminary professor degrading Robert Schuller. I was smart enough not to show any displeasure to the couple. But her comment, lodged in my mind, in part, caused me to go back and question my own thinking later. In other words, even with "education," I am thankful I felt open to learning from all people, including my own parishioners.

A few years later, I happened to tune into Robert Schuller, and I found that, ultimately, he made me think of Jesus. Jesus spoke to the people on their level about their problems, and Dr. Schuller spoke to the current problems that people of today were having, such as how to live with confidence in home and career, how to live free of fear and worry, personal power issues, joy in living, how to have peace of mind and, above all, faith—how to move with genuine, practical faith in life's challenges. He spoke to my issues, I found, and I was refreshed with new hope after tuning in. He did not speak traditional biblical language, no more than Jesus spoke like Moses, but he did the work of the good news.

Schuller moved into teaching people to love themselves. Love themselves? That was not how the church had controlled people for ages. It had taught them to despise themselves, degrade themselves, have no opinions, be powerless. That is what I had learned to do, and true to church doctrine, that was a cornerstone in my own ministry—the depravity of man. Schuller understood what he was doing and its relationship to what the church had done over the centuries—he called his self-love theology a new reformation. As my book goes to press, the Crystal Cathedral is going through serious problems, as is Dr. Robert Schuller, but my now positive appreciation for him remains strong, no matter how these things turn out.

Yet officials in the churches spoke out and declared Robert Schuller a heretic, a non-Christian. Only when Billy Graham took the heat and said Robert Schuller was okay did some of the criticism begin to let off.

I ran across a portion of an interview of Billy Graham by Robert Schuller, and it reveals even Billy Graham, who had much to lose but is admired because he followed truth as best he knew it, shifted his theology and opened his mind to a bigger God. Here is a portion of the interview.

> Billy Graham: And that's what God is doing today. He's calling people out of the world for His name. Whether they come from the Muslim world, or the Buddhist world, or the Christian world, or the non-believing world, they are members of the Body of Christ, because they've been called by God. They may not even know the name of Jesus, but they know in their hearts that they need something that they don't have, and they turn to the only light that they have, and I think they are saved, and that they're going to be with us in heaven.

> Robert Schuller: What, what I hear you saying, that it's possible for Jesus Christ to come into human hearts and soul and life, even if they've been born in darkness and have never had exposure to the Bible. Is that a correct interpretation of what you're saying?

> Graham: Yes, it is, because I believe that. I've met people in various parts of the world in tribal situations, that they have never seen a Bible or heard about a Bible, and never heard of Jesus, but they've believed in their hearts that there was a God, and they've tried to live a life that was quite apart from the surrounding community in which they lived.

Schuller: [Schuller trips over his tongue for a moment, his face beaming, then says] I'm so thrilled to hear you say this. There's a wideness in God's mercy.

Graham: There is. There definitely is.

My story at this point is about much more than Robert Schuller. It is about a mindset, about programming in religion, and how difficult it may be for any of us to break into new and better grounding of our faith, as it was for me. Kudos for Billy Graham, but I don't know of many people who paid attention to the dramatic point he was making in relationship to his former preaching. Many churches have tried to keep the viewpoint he developed late in his life hush-hush quiet.

Opening myself to a greater faith that included preachers such as Robert Schuller and motivational writers such as Napoleon Hill was moving me forward on my spiritual quest. I was getting closer and closer to my unseen goal. I was doing what anyone must who wants to walk more fully on his or her spiritual consciousness—that is, to become more and more open, like a blossoming flower in the desert. I had learned this back in Goleta when I had begun reading about Martin Luther, but I was still having to rediscover the importance of an open mind in advancing spiritually. Openness did not mean accepting every idea that came my way. I remained discerning while I challenged my own ideas, seeing if they would hold up under scrutiny.

These non-mainstream teachers were giving me help and direction through non-church avenues because these people, truly, were spreading the good news, the gospel, although I had never heard anyone say that. It was a novel ideal but true to the ministry and model of the life of Jesus. They were doing what the church should have been doing. And when their messages give people solid hope and direction, isn't that good? Why make the word "gospel" so churchy and theological? Why relegate it to something only about dying and going to a happy-hunting-ground heaven? Why not do what Jesus did and make it practical for the everyday life?

Wasn't Wayne Dyer giving people good news, helping to let them enter into a new experience of heavenly joy right here in this lifetime, I asked myself.

But I didn't want to put Jesus's name in what Dyer and the others like him were doing. I saw that, after two thousand years, people were using the name Jesus to mean whatever they wanted. There is no copyright to his name, and they used it to validate all sorts of ideas, including the orthodox doctrines that emerged over the four hundred years after his death in the Greek- and Latin-speaking world of the Roman Empire. But as this broke upon the Enlightenment and democracy, and the ability of religious people to start their own religions around the world, Jesus was represented as one who stood for one thing here, another thing there, and confusion resulted. Each religious system mixed its own ideas with Biblical verses to propagate an image of Jesus of its own making for its own purposes. And so we lost a sense of the real Jesus and of the good work he did.

Some people thought if they held the right beliefs they would be saved. That is, rather than having a spiritual relationship with God, they needed to believe in specific doctrines about God in order to be saved: Jesus came from heaven; Jesus died on the cross for our sins; God is omniscient, omnipotent, and omnipresent; God is love; the Bible is the Word of God. They had to believe the Creed and believe in the sacraments. The list goes on to fill many doctrine books, and each Christian religion has its own variations. I even remember going to a church that had no pianos, organs, or any musical instruments. To have a musical instrument in church was a sin in that religion. Was it? Does it really matter? Is wrangling over these kinds of details going to help us on our spiritual path?

What Billy Graham said in the quoted passage agrees with this. The key to salvation lies not in all those doctrines or in your choice of religion or even in a Jesus or the Bible but simply in believing in God.

Take "God is love" from the previous list of right beliefs. It is one thing to believe God is love but another to love God and feel his love to us and act in accordance with that love filling our whole being. When believing in doctrine is the ultimate litmus test of what makes a believer, the facts we believe become more important than how we feel in our hearts As I continued exploring the non-mainstream teachers and their philosophies, I saw that that reliance on doctrine led to a sense of one person or religion being better than another and to division among people of the world. Those who relied on their belief in doctrines to be saved easily fell into self-righteous separation from those who did not believe as they did and, then, readily excluded them.

The Bible passage that I found helpful in dealing with the situation in Goleta came back to me now in full force as I wrestled with this problem of belief in doctrine versus God. Jesus said:

By their fruits you will know them.

Only a message from the Bible could have fully moved my heart as it did because of my love and respect for the Scriptures. It opened the door for me to look at the gospel differently. The gospel was good news, and if it was genuine gospel, it would produce good things in people's lives, genuine, authentic positive effects from the heart. We could each make our own list, but I thought of confidence, fearlessness, peace of mind, courage, compassion, ease of forgiveness, joy, and unconditional love emerging naturally from life. What stood for truth was no longer specific doctrines everyone agreed upon but the life of the heart connected to the greater Spirit, flowing with goodness into the earth like a fresh stream. What we did—the results, our fruits, our acting with Spirit—mattered more than what doctrines we held. Simply believing in doctrines did not create this fruit of the Spirit. Indeed, Jesus was crucified by those who held to doctrines and teachings and rules as the true way of God on earth. Good fruit is its own verification. I think it is clear that the ultimate fruit, according to Jesus, is love to God and neighbor, loving especially the enemy, and forgiving self and everyone else. And for me, the new world I moved into, theologically, bore good fruit, and hence it became the bearer of the gospel.

This reorganization of my understanding greatly helped me to appreciate fully this new body of thinking by those I had previously considered outsiders. As much praise as I have for seminary, the professors shortchanged us by teaching us never to speak of our experiences in life and never to focus on the spiritual experience of church members.

And yet, the New Testament was nothing if not filled with stories of spiritual experiences of people. That is the key—the results. Some of the so-called heretics manifested good in their lives and in the people they taught. Some of the orthodox were not manifesting good things at all, but self-righteousness, discrimination, lack of forgiveness, and other life-destroying qualities. And so today. What served the people best in dealing with world problems, personal problems, personal aspirations, health, and understanding came from good fruit-bearing work of the gospel. What promoted love, acceptance, and compassion? Belief in the love of God.

I was discovering that our spiritual work here must be something relevant, meaningful, and powerful that creates a new heaven for people on earth NOW, as Eckhart Tolle teaches. And we did not always need to mention Jesus's name in doing our good work; any more than Mother Theresa did every time she served a dying man, woman, or child in his or her poverty. To do so for us would only serve to confuse those wanting to do good and would play into the hands of egocentric religionists and moralists who would twist it to suit their purposes.

The more I opened myself to spiritual possibilities outside the traditional church's teachings, the more I saw that the spiritual world is above any one religion and that unity comes when we get the best from our religions and move through them into the fullness of the presence of God. This leaves room for a world of different religious practices. They need not merge, and we need not leave our religions at all; we just use them differently. Jesus is the religion I know best, and I found he teaches this very idea. "Love your neighbor as yourself," he taught, and both "neighbor" and "yourself" can be a Moslem, Buddhist, Taoist, Hindu, any religious believer, or even an atheist or pagan.

When they say there are many avenues to the end goal of enlightenment, I think of how Washington, DC, is laid out. All streets from the outlying areas meet in the center where the capital grounds and parks are. Likewise, the different paths of other religions can take their followers to meet all in that glorious center of oneness with God. And if Christians are to help people find that center, they must do so with their actions. By the fruits of our goodness will we be known.

Everyone is progressing to the same center—just on different paths, at different points, at different speeds. Who knows what unlikely person or event will carry each of us forward, one step closer to our goal? For me, one youth, barely out of high school, came along my path and started a chain of changes in my spiritual quest. Presenting me with a set of Tony Robbins tapes at a crucial moment, he brought me something that would trouble me at first, then cause me to resolve the contradictions I saw, and finally, inspire me to become more open and keep me moving into new realms and ever closer to that center goal.

CHAPTER 17

Every single experience in my life, right up to this
day, was something I needed to go through in order
to get to be here now, writing these words.

Wayne Dyer

Man's real life consists of a complex of inexorable
opposites, day and night, birth and death, happiness
and misery, good and evil ... Life is a battleground. It
always has been and always will be: and if it were not
so, existence would come to an end.

Carl Gustav Jung

I came into the world with an attraction for religion, and I was brought up religious. But my greater mission from early childhood on was to find the truth, the ultimate life of life. I had thought religion would lead me to truth, but I discovered that, sometimes, the church keeps us from the very reality of life. Religions have a tendency to encase themselves in historical boxes, that is doctrines, and teach that to be saved one must climb in the box and believe those doctrines. Their focus on rules and right thinking and proper behavior often overwhelm any ideas about spirituality or connecting with God. Aiming for extreme morality or holiness, many times, leads to a self-centeredness that actually keeps God out of the picture. Instead, the spiritual life fully connected to God lets us breathe freely, fills us with compassion, love, and care for others as well as self, and gives us a healthy sense of self.

The truth, I found, is greater than any one religion can hold and, yet, close at hand. Reality was already inside of me all along because reality is the Spirit, and Spirit resides in me. But the challenge was to get to it.

Finding a spiritual connection had little to do with joining the right church or religion, leading the holiest life, finding the perfect cave in the Himalayas for meditation, or discovering the latest spiritual fad. It simply required me to learn how to be myself and, as a first step, drop trying to fit into someone else's idea of what is right and wrong for me. I had to unwind layers of ideas, rather than find something or someone out there in the blue to add to my life, and let my own desires pull me forward. This was not easy when voices from every corner of the earth tell us how to live, what to do, what to think, how to behave, and what to believe.

We cannot silence those voices, but we can decide whether to listen to them and how much of their advice to accept. I learned that and gained what good I could from some of what I heard, but ultimately, I set much aside to listen to my own inner voice as my primary guide. I was given a brain to think and a heart to feel. I also inherited some glaring defects to heal. And I encountered horrible loss and grief. All these things served me and propelled me forward. I did not want to live in the pain of grief forever, and I did not want to carry personal defects forever. Finding ways to heal the wounds in my soul also pointed me to spirituality as reality.

In my hunt for the reality of life, I also questioned my tendency for perfectionism. Eventually, I understood that if I continued trying to *be* perfect or do "it" perfectly, I would never find what I ultimately wanted. I learned to do my best, and that is all I can do. Trying to do more was wasting time and energy and piling frustration into my psyche. I needed to lighten up and enjoy what I could. As Martin Luther said, "If we are not allowed to laugh in heaven, I don't want to go there." I like his attitude—let's lighten up, not take ourselves too seriously, be comfortable with who we are in our individuality. Dwelling, instead, on our grief, on our shortcomings and sins, or on any health, relationship, or money problem will only make problems worse. Lightening up has the best chance for all of us to make success.

And, so, I made a conscious choice—to be grateful and happy rather than to hold onto resentment and sorrow. I began by expressing my gratitude for where I was at the moment in both spiritual and material areas. Each time I did this, my thankfulness reminded me of the joy I already held and brought more of the same to me.

Within this frame of gratitude and lightheartedness, I made my search for a truth beyond what religions were giving me.

So how did I find what I have found in spiritual reality?

First, I began by asking questions. I was always a seeker, and the tragic wreck when I lost the love of my life catapulted me in my quest for spiritual truth. It brought out doubts and questions I never would have confronted without the extreme nature of the accident. They gnawed at me, and I had to find the answers. I could set them aside for a while, but they remained and, always at the right time, rose up to remind me to continue searching. My intense desire for truth set me on a lifelong search. And the Spirit was right there with me, showing me the way, putting the perfect circumstance in my lap, nudging me in the right direction.

Recognizing the gifts Spirit was giving me took time. They didn't come with a big sign, "Go with this person" or "Pay attention to this" or "Here's your next step." I had to learn to pay attention and have confidence in taking a next step. More than anything, I had to quiet my mind so that I could feel or hear something move inside me. When I turned off my analytical mind, Spirit could enter and be heard. This wasn't a voice talking to me; it was more of a feeling, an urge, the sense that I needed to take a certain action. Being an avid reader, I found bookstores especially helpful to me. Several times, I "just happened" into the right book totally by accident. Other times, my car seemed to drive and park itself, and lo and behold, I would just happen into something I needed.

All of those synchronistic moments came to me because I had opened myself to letting them happen; I had asked. I like the way Jesus put it when he said seek and we will find. I needed to keep looking for it. That took time.

And I had to get very hungry for the answers. I needed that drive—a rabid hunger for truth—to guide me and to keep me on track, especially when I hit the barriers of my closed mindedness. I came to see that when I fell into a problem that overwhelmed me, the Spirit was using the situation to get me to search for a higher way for my life. It signaled I had to reexamine some of my beliefs or reconsider the direction I was going. I needed to probe deep within, be sure of what I wanted, and let the Spirit through my quieted mind guide me.

My drive to find, again, the spiritual high carried me forward. I learned, and that meant making mistakes and then trying again. As Babe Ruth said, "Every strike out brings me closer to the next home run." Giving up never entered my thoughts.

I found help in the motivational movement, but sometimes I wasted time and money in gurus who promised instant, fast-food-type fixes to problems, instant answers to gain riches and wonderful relationships. I had to sort out the wheat from the chaff—although one person's chaff might be wheat for another. It is all part of steps along the path, if we let it be. My openness always walked hand in hand with common sense, and I recognized the charlatans—eventually—and then moved on, ever searching. When I felt discouraged, I remembered Jesus's words: "Come to me all who are weary and heavy laden." And I would step aside, relax, and rest for a while.

After I abandoned Plan A with the Campus Crusaders, my path to spiritual enlightenment never again took the fast track. It became a process that I could not rush. I had to let it unfold as Spirit knew best for me. My world-famous and late seminary professor, Dr. Gerhard O. Forde, of Luther Seminary, who arranged for my entrance into PhD studies at Marquette University, said in his humble, Norwegian way, with very little expression, "Terry, someone said to me when I started my doctorate that its greatest value is not what you learn but what you become." I was on a lifelong journey to become a better me, and I decided to relax and enjoy the journey as much as I would enjoy the destination.

Second, I discovered that no one religion or theological agenda held the final answer, but each could help with a road map or provide steppingstones along the way. I never changed my religion, but I did change churches several times, and each one built on what I had gained before, giving me fresh goals and ideals to help me move forward. Standing on the shoulders of my religion, I was moving into my own eternal divine life. But as much as I loved my church, it was a second love. The Spirit was my first. Love God with all your heart, soul, strength, and mind, the master taught, and so I did.

Once my mind had grasped the idea of spiritual enlightenment, I saw that I needed to make my experience match that concept. I wasn't yet living it to the full, especially in my chosen church. When I did find a community, a church that supported my search for the experience, and it was by sheer luck or, rather, synchronicity, my advancement moved me forward with exponential speed. As Ernest Holmes said, "Everyone, while remaining individual, shall find a more complete expression in and among all other individuals." Although I recognized the problems with the church of my upbringing and its firm grip of outdated doctrines, I gained too much from my association with a church community to cast it aside. Without a faith community, my spiritual progress was less effective.

But I know many have taken different paths involving organized religion. As Ms. Lessing quotes respected Vietnamese spiritual writer, Thich Nhat Hanh, "Many people are so turned off by religions—their seemingly arbitrary moral codes, the boundless hypocrisies between word and deed, the arcane rituals—that they have acquired a resistance to spirituality itself."

I have thought long and hard about the dark side of religion. I recognized it long ago, but I still feel awkward and incomplete without religion in my life, and the way I deal with it is that I have found a church I can sink my teeth into and fully value. Because it offers so much good for my life, it is my job to give thanks, appreciate it, and avoid getting caught up in any human foibles or weaknesses that arise. On a more practical or mundane level, I gain supportive relationships in the church, economic and practical advice, and a place to serve and give to and through. But finding and expressing my spirituality in the Spirit is my number one concern. Fortunately, my religion through this church supports my own spirituality, encourages my own thinking, lets me follow what I see and feel, and agrees with me that God permeates every single one of us.

Third, I discovered the power in meditation. I had to learn to quiet the mind, stop thinking, and sink into the subconscious of life every day. Everyday, I needed the peace meditation brought. It allowed me to find inspiration, to have confidence in following what I believed Spirit was guiding me to do, and to connect with God. Ultimately, I found a meditation group, and all of us agree our meditations are all more powerful when we meet occasionally for a common mediation experience.

Meditation, alone, did not bring spiritual consciousness in its fullness, but I needed the quiet as a foundation for the other to follow. Meditation and prayer go together. Some people teach to pray about others first, to get love flowing. Sometimes I think of loved ones and transfer spiritual consciousness from and through my spirit to theirs. It is amazing how someone I haven't heard from in a long time calls after I have done this. Others let the Spirit prompt them by showing them someone's face or name, which I also do. But my method is my personal method, like my taste in dining; it works for me. Each person has different needs and preferences and styles and must find what works for him or her. The specifics of the method do not matter; practicing meditation does. If one is hungry for truth and life and the Spirit, meditation will provide a means for finding them.

True meditation allowed me to find God—not God out there in the blue somewhere but God who has always been with me, for me, around me, above me, below me, and most of all, in me. I meditated just to quiet all the outward stuff so what was inside and has always been there could enlighten me. This is called spiritual enlightenment—not a Spirit out there coming to me as much as the Spirit in me getting out from behind my egoistic dark curtain. As Ernest Holmes said, "Your endeavor, then, is not so much to find God as it is to realize His Presence and to understand that this Presence is always with you. Your outward search for God culminates in the greatest of all possible discoveries—the finding of Him at the center of you own being. Life flows up from within you."

It does exactly that, I am finding more and more and more, and it is wonderful.

And now, the most important discovery I made in my journey so far I present in the last chapter. It is my final word in this book, but it comes before all others.

CHAPTER 18

The weak can never forgive. Forgiveness is the attribute of the strong.

Mahatma Gandhi

As I saw the spirituality path opening before me, I realized the resentment I was harboring against some who had hurt me emotionally was barring my advancement. I had submerged some of the painful issues and kept distance from some people, but now, they were rising up in my mind so that was I seeing the problems and the people and how much I disliked or resented them. And their memory or false reality in my mind blocked my way. I could see the way ahead, but I could not go forward without dealing with these people. I would have to forgive them all.

The teaching of Jesus according to Matthew came to me, that if we don't forgive others, we ourselves are not forgiven. But, too often, the church taught that Christ forgave people, which made dealing with this part of Scriptures awkward or, even, unnecessary. People knew it was there but rationalized it away. We would try to forgive ourselves and others later, when we were ready; meanwhile, Christ could take care of the situation for us.

But the teaching in the Sermon on the Mount clearly told us that, unless we do forgive all others of anything and everything, we ourselves are not forgiven. As Edmund Burke, philosopher and politician in the eighteenth century, in speaking on our failure to forgive, said, "[it] was never a rational thing; it distorts all the faculties of the human mind, it perverts them, it leaves a man no longer in the free use of his reason, it puts him in to confusion." I agree, and I will show why we must forgive all and what to do that works.

Founder of modern psychology, Sigmund Freud brought out the influence of our parents and gave people permission to deflect their own guilt for their activities onto their parents or other external circumstances. In the end, the actions of parents or anyone else makes no difference to us if we are to free ourselves. Even if parents are guilty, we must release them. To be free, we must look back through the heart and eyes of compassion, love, and forgiveness if we are to move forth in life with power and freedom. We can unconsciously cast blame on someone twenty-four hours a day—and be right about it. But that does not release us from their continued power over us.

This is not an easy subject, I know. Once I learned the value of therapy, about the time I was being introduced to motivational speakers, I was eager to go through the process. My therapist helped me see that I could blame my parents and a whole list of people for certain destructive behaviors in my life. But the therapist told me nothing about forgiveness. He did not teach me that holding onto my grudges, keeping blame alive, allowed these people to lurk in the shadows of my current life, often hidden but still there. Although he helped me improve my sense of self, he did not take me to the next level, that is, to find who had harmed me and to forgive them completely.

It is not that I went around armed with grudges. I had become fairly happy and did not spend time thinking of people who had hurt me. But, nevertheless, in certain situations, my lack of forgiveness made me ineffective and powerless. I think guilt and fear are two fingers on the same hand, and I had some fears in my life, and I trace them to this issue of unforgiveness.

Nor did my therapist have the tools to show me how to forgive. I truly believe the reason we have not gone after the guilt raging in our souls, the reason we have deflected it onto others and denied it in ourselves, is because we simply do not know how to get rid of it. The task seems impossible so we pretend the problem does not exist. And, of course, it does remain, festering in places unseen and holding us back from advancing in our spiritual journey. When I am sharing with people, this one area brings out the fastest and biggest objections. Such strong resistance merely shows me that guilt still lies hidden within them because of their refusal to forgive, and that, in turn, keeps them from the wonderful experience of a connection with God.

Despite the protections I had put up that kept me from forgiving others, I learned that *forgiveness is absolutely and totally critical if we do not want to remain stunted in our spiritual growth.* Nothing else matters as far as reaching genuine and full spiritual consciousness. We can meditate all day long. We can talk of loving our neighbors and ourselves. We can go to retreats, seminars, churches, spirituality conferences, read books, do good works and more. But until we conquer the barrier that calls for forgiveness of self and others, we are stymied. I have done all these things, and I do not deny their value. But conquering this one final area knocked down enormous roadblocks to my goal.

Knowing that I could not continue on a path toward infinite love if I still held negative thoughts about people of my past, I had but one choice. So, as much as it might hurt me to begin letting certain people off the hook in my consciousness, accepting them fully, and even coming to love and appreciate them, I decided I would do so. And I emphasize the word "decided" in what I did. I never forced myself. I realized what I needed to do, and then, I wanted to do it. Commanding, demanding, forcing, condemning, guilt-provoking, or any other attempts that work against our inner desires will not produce the honest, clean, and clear results that advance our spiritual progress. Dragging a load of invisible guilt truly stops our souls from flowing the rich honey of love they hold. And if we have not forgiven people that we resent or who have harmed us, we are guilty.

I also found that sincere Christians had a tendency to think they had forgiven others, but they had done so only in the Christian club, so to speak. They still held superiority feelings towards outsiders, which did not embrace the fully forgiving attitude Jesus had taught.

Recently, I talked with a relative who has attended a good, upstanding, and successful church in her town. As we began to talk about our childhoods and churches and how we felt, it was so clear that she was still under a terrible power of guilt in her mind and life. She hadn't done things well enough, she said. When she thought of God, she was still a bit afraid. This is a story I believe can be repeated by many: We think we don't measure up. Guilt is no small issue.

Nor is forgiveness. And it requires a huge step to move forward with it, over the guilt that keeps us from our goal.

Marianne Williamson advances forgiveness so that it is not based on anyone's apology but on higher consciousness in the Spirit: "Traditionally, we think of forgiveness as something we are to do when we see guilt in someone ... It is our function to see through the illusion of guilt, to the innocence that lies beyond ... all the rest must be forgotten." Her thought is close to what Jesus said when he told his followers to love their enemies. In other words, to forgive is not just to accept an apology but to release the person completely from accountability to us and to begin to look at his or her pure heart with compassion and love.

My life has had little steps of positive change whenever I met someone who looked into my heart and saw purity and goodness, which brought those qualities to the surface. Approaching everyone in this way—not to hold anything against anyone but to look into each heart with compassion and see the fullness of God in its potential—means to live in forgiveness. Whenever I do that, look upon the other's innocence, I help release that person from his or her bondages, and I release anyone else who has trespassed again me

All the meditation in the world will not achieve our highest potential until we encounter this critical area—face our guilt, resentment, and superiority feelings and fully forgive all. It starts with each one of us, one at a time. Self-help books tell us what we should and shouldn't do in these areas, but in my experience, they do not always give us tools to do it. Knowing I should build a house does not help me build one. I need someone to show me how. Being told I should love so and so is just a vapid law unless someone shows me how. And being told it is good to forgive everyone is an empty platitude until someone shows me how to do it, shows by his or her own life and explains a system or tool for doing it. We need good, humble teachers who do practice forgiveness themselves.

We need teachers like Jesus who not only tell us what needs to be done but who also do it to us and start the ball rolling. Upon the cross, he said, "Father, forgive them, for they know not what they do." What was he teaching? How important was forgiving others for him? Can any of us imagine a Jesus who would have died with a grudge or hatred on his lips towards his accusers and crucifiers? In other words, he taught by example.

Some of us ask, what good did that do? He got himself killed. One man I know, a religious leader from whom I have learned some good things, said it was the dumbest thing Jesus ever did. This man was trying to make sense of Jesus's crucifixion, but he still did not know the need to forgive others, and he was a recognized teacher in the world of spirituality—which reinforces my point about how critical it is we visit this issue. Not everyone knows it or teaches it. He did not see that Jesus would even give his life to teach this point. If forgiveness of others is one of the most important bridges to spiritual consciousness, perhaps teaching by the ultimate example and hanging on the cross with a forgiving heart was one of the greatest things he ever did.

Like too many people, this man failed to understand the power that guilt holds over us—and the power that forgiveness offers to overcome that barrier. Time and again, I saw people suffering in their refusal to forgive. Once I was talking with a woman of Chinese origin in her apartment in Seattle as she was buying health insurance from me. We were in a discussion when I said that forgiveness is not about letting others off the hook; it is about letting ourselves off the hook, releasing ourselves from their power. She looked at me as if she was in a trance, as if God had just spoken to her.

"I never knew that," she finally said.

I had thought everyone knew that. I was as stunned by her profound reaction as she was. Later, I contemplated our discussion, and I had an image of each of us dragging many, many people along behind us—some alive, some dead, all not forgiven. They are heavy, and they are holding us back from moving effectively in life, and certainly from leaping to the next stone in our spiritual consciousness development. To hold a grudge, to want revenge, to be under the control of the memories of our parents in a bad way, for example, or anyone else, even if just resting under the surface of our consciousness, is giving power to those people over us.

To forgive is to cut the cords and release ourselves. But if you can't, you can't, and I will deal with that in a moment.

So as a first point of application, forgiveness means release. For Jesus, "Father, forgive them for they know not what they do," means, "Release me from their power in my soul to want revenge. They did hurt me, Father; this is not easy. They are killing me, destroying my good reputation, making me into a criminal. It hurts, truly. I am not passive but really feel this, Father. I thirst. And remember, Father, I know they still do not have knowledge of spiritual consciousness. They are still caught in their egos. Oh my Father, have compassion on them. Bless them. Release them from their hatred of me, just as I release me from bitterness towards them. As I pass along to you, Father, I do not carry anything to you but the very best blessing upon them to you. Please receive my forgiveness towards them."

There, in Jesus, is a teacher who leads by example into higher spiritual consciousness.

If we do not release those who sin against us, we are not released. We are holding onto them in our consciousness and letting them have power over us. (In Greek, the word for forgiveness is *aphiemi*, which means to let go, send away, cancel, pardon, abandon, and similar terms.) To forgive those who do something wrong to us is to release them from controlling our emotions, and emotions are at the seat of what we do. They control our outcomes, the life we end up having.

Without forgiving every single one completely, I really haven't forgiven anyone yet. Why? Because I remain in bondage. It doesn't matter if I drag one or one hundred behind me; I still drag a load.

Holding onto my grudge with even one holds me back from advancing on my spiritual path.

To forgive people that do not affect me personally, I find, is not hard. But that is not really forgiveness. I can forgive Hitler for Dachau because I didn't have any relatives killed there. That's easy. But when it gets personal, when I find I had grudges against friends, co-workers, neighbors, or family who hurt me, for example, the process is more difficult. I would like to say that I have forgiven all against whom I held a grudge, that I have finished forgiving, but no. The Spirit, on occasion, brings up new situations to act upon, revives old people from out of the closets of darkness and into my awareness. At times, visions of some wrong I did to someone decades ago have awakened me in the night, and I know I must take action and forgive. I might try to find that person and ask forgiveness for any harm I did. Or, knowing contact could do more harm than good, I just meditate on it and let it go.

I have learned how to forgive people who have stolen from me. When I see them, I look them in the eye as a friend, with compassion. If they had taken my last morsel or last penny, I might have had to revisit my entire process, for this does not come easy. But once we get used to the feeling we gain when we ferret out all wrongdoing against us and release it to the higher power and source of our life, it feels so good we never want to lose it.

Once I took this step completely—dealing with everyone I held negative feelings for—I made my most accelerated advances into spiritual consciousness. As I let some people who had done some nasty things to me go, I was actually letting myself go free in my soul, and the release had some wonderful repercussions I had not anticipated. My grudges had hidden some inner guilt and the reasons for some fears I held. When I let go of the first, the others fell away as well. Once I conquered my barrier of unforgiveness, my fears began to fall like tears of rain.

I have found that Christians can be very stubborn in forgiving. And this may be true of other religious people as well, but I am more familiar with the Christian arena. Some, so sure that their religion or church is the right one, look down on those in other denominations. I've heard people say, "We feel we have just a bit more truth than others." Our feeling of superiority keeps us from even considering forgiving others; if we forgave, we would let "those people" stand on the same level with us. "Good Christians" also tend to underline sins, like fornication, in our Bibles and look askance at the folks whose morals we don't think match our high ones in that regard. But when it comes to our sins that reveal unforgiving attitudes, like gossip, slander, hatred, bitterness, and even judgementalism, we let ourselves off the hook.

Some claim they don't need to forgive themselves; they already have Jesus's forgiveness—this is why he died for them, they say. So they start deflecting all their personal responsibility upon him. But "forgiveness of mankind, of everyone in every circumstance, is our ticket to Heaven, our only way home," says Marianne Williamson. What she means is that while Jesus did forgive on the cross, he didn't pick up anyone's ticket to heaven. Wouldn't that be a cheap gospel?

No, he was trying to start a wave, where we would start forgiving everyone and spread that lifestyle—so healthy in soul and mind—into a life on Earth he called the Kingdom of God. Jesus was showing us the what and the how. He was not doing it for us so we could run around and bask in a shallow idea of grace and then look down on the neighbor of a different religious persuasion. Here was the teacher getting down and dirty, as dirty as it gets. He died to start a process that he wanted us to carry on, learning from his example how to forgive. We may not be called to a cross, but we are called to forgive all, for until we experience forgiveness, we know not what we are doing.

And that "all" includes ourselves. It does no good to try to have a wonderful new relationship with God and move forward along a path to higher spiritual consciousness if we harbor unforgiveness in our heart towards anyone, anyone at all, including ourselves.

Often, we forget about forgiving that most important person, our self. We tend to blame others for our problems, encouraged by therapists, the media, and society in general. The easy way points a finger at those who did us wrong, and we avoid facing our part in whatever happened. We all want to be right and believe we are good, so our egos do their best to make us feel secure by casting the other in a shadow and us in the light. But deep down, we know we hold some responsibility for our actions. And when we fail to recognize our guilt, fail to accept responsibility, fail to acknowledge our part—however small—we lose our opportunity to forgive ourselves.

We must forgive ourselves as we forgive others, just as we must love ourselves as we love our neighbor. Holding the least feeling of guilt within us keeps us from the ultimate love, our unity with God. The way to love is through forgiveness.

Wanting to forgive marks the first step. But actually granting forgiveness to others and self represents a huge leap over a gorge for many people; it is one of the hardest things they think they have to do. But … no one has to forgive.

Someone asked the pastor, Rev. Dr. Kathianne Lewis, in a class, "Do I have to forgive?"

And she said, "No, you don't have to do anything. The issue is, what do you want? Do you want to be free, to have a wonderful life? Full life? Are you hungry for spiritual awareness in your life consistently, or do you want to go on the way you are? Either way is OK. It is up to each one of you."

But if we feel we cannot forgive, what then? Here is the critical key that can set us free from guilt.

If we can't do it, we turn it over to God. We can do that, with help. If we can't even do that, then we turn over *that* problem—the problem that we can't turn it over—and keep going until we find our sweet spot. It sounds silly, but really, it works. In our mind and prayer, we say, "OK, Great One, God, I can't forgive so and so, but I can release myself from this inability, and turn it over to you." And then we check into our souls several times a day, because if God is alive, he will work in our hearts to change them and give us this ability. If we can't release it to God, we take the next step backwards. We say, "God, I can't release this person, and I can't release my inability to you, but I release myself from my inability to release." We keep going until we find how many steps back it takes to release to God. If we can't forgive—and most of us can't, not right away—we just accept that and place our difficulty in God's hands.

Now, with this method, when we can't forgive, what happens? We don't feel guilty. We don't act helpless. We just release ourselves from our inability. This point is so crucial, I hope readers mark it, copy it, make it personal. We turn our inability over to a higher power and watch God at work in us. The key is to stay open and wait for the help God will bring. We say, "Okay God, I need to forgive, to clear away the clutter keeping me from spiritual consciousness. But I can't. So I am giving it to you. And I am going to keep my eye on you and check in to see how you are doing in my life."

Then snappo! One day we find we have released that person. Done deal. No more guilt for you. Just watch, and you will see.

ᴈ

I started the story of my own spiritual journey in this book with the tragic event that put me more intensely in the spiritual path. Nancy was killed, and she was the love of my life. Her favorite Bible passage was John 15. If I heard her say it once, I heard her say it a dozen times until it got totally embedded in my mind: Jesus is the vine, we are the branches, meaning we are one with him, we are of his nature, we bear fruit or good works through him, all of us together. Nancy, in her advanced spirituality, knew she was one with God. Most of the rest of us knew the passage but operated as if we were still separate from one another or even in some sort of competition with each other. But for her, we were one. We were knitted together by the Spirit. Individuals? Of course.

I didn't see what she saw then. It has taken me a lifetime, but now I do. Thank you, Nancy and Christ in Nancy.

Nancy remains one of the most wonderful people I have ever known. I say this not lightly but from reflection, and she knew she could never be separated from God, even by death. I knew her well, and there was not one person in the world who had sinned against her she had not released. She herself was a free person.

A question I am asked is, "How can you forgive a person who purposely sped his car out of control on a wet pavement and killed your bride of one day?"

My thoughts and actions come after taking step after step into the invisible spiritual life over many years.

Forgiveness is releasing to the Spirit. It is acknowledging there is a higher reality that will do the judging. It is surrender to God, and without it, we fall short of living in spiritual consciousness. In my soul and mind, I have released the person who slammed into Nancy and me, and in so doing, I have released myself to continue on my spiritual journey. Sometimes I have to do it again. Sometimes I can feel an anger rise up, and I know that is an indication of grief and the small, egoic me and not the large me in Christ. So I do the forgiveness process once again. If I can't forgive at that moment, I release my inability to the Spirit within me, God. And sure enough, God comes through, and ultimately, I can release him again. I went through that process many times as I wrote this book, especially the first chapter where I relived the entire accident over again and gave up the reality of what could have been life with her. I am now very happy with my life.

Because I aspire to forgive fully any who have harmed me and have followed my own path in my spiritual search, some would say I am not religious. Well, what is it to be religious? To live as Jesus did? To be happy? To be free? Not to worry about what people think and live my life as my own conscience tells me? Yes to all. The answers revolve around what Jesus taught—to look for the best in people, avoiding slander, criticism, and a fixation the moralism religion is famous for. And I see "religious" as going beyond those points—teaching when called upon and not necessarily what the church determined seventeen hundred years ago but my truth as I know it.

The Bible authorizes so much more joy in life than typical religions say—to have fun, to have wonderful relationships in addition to religious ones, and to enjoy everyone, from the simple and uneducated who have a great heart to the high and mighty who are lonely at the top. But if I hold a grudge against the young man who drove the car into us, who is in bondage? I am. I am beholden to him. Early on, after the accident, every time I would think of him, I would get a bad feeling. Thoughts of revenge would overcome me, and I would surrender my choice to live freely and fully. My own dark side would rise up and take over my mind. In holding unforgiveness and anger for this person, I would give him control over my life, letting him and those thoughts snuff the joy out of it. I gained nothing good. Yes, I still think about him. Someone pressured me to be real, and this is real. I harbor no resentment towards him at all. Many others affected by this tragedy have also moved on and made the most of it, making themselves better people.

My forgiving the young man also opened me to a fuller perspective of what happened: I could have been the one causing such a tragic loss. I think back to what some of my teen friends and I did with our cars when I was younger, and it could have been me running into a newly married couple and killing the bride. There, but for the grace of God, go I.

So who is it we ultimately release when we forgive another? Ourselves.

We continue under bondage—we are not released—until we release that one, whoever it may be. This is not about a Christianity that gets our ticket punched for a trip to heaven when we die. It is about the passion of Jesus for a better world, for justice, for what he called the Kingdom of God.

It is kind of like the old jailer who got sick of tending the jail, feeding the prisoner, and emptying his latrine pail day after day after day for years. Finally, one day he took the key, opened the door, and said to the man, "Let's both get out of here and go get new jobs." That's what it is to let someone free whom we've held in our mental prison of unforgiveness.

So as Marianne Williamson says, "What we give to others, we give to ourselves. What we withhold from others, we withhold from ourselves." Hence, we validate the other person in our hearts, and we thus validate ourselves. Forgiveness is a higher spirit of consciousness towards all people.

Forgiveness is the new human community, unifying us all, and, thus, gives us what the church fails to provide. The church was not meant to be just a separate religious institution. Biblically, it was the human community of people who were learning to move beyond their fearful, separate egos into the power of acceptance, peace, patience, kindness, and authentic love for each and every one. It was meant to be a guiding light for the people searching for the good news, a connection with God, a spiritual consciousness.

I sensed from early on that the church of my upbringing did not provide that kind of guidance to the people. It provided community of sorts but not one that truly led us to a higher spiritual experience with God. And my experience on the gurney in the hospital told me I should expect that or, at least, to aim for that. So I sought it elsewhere, first in the groups in Eugene and Goleta and then in my academic training. But none worked, not completely. Yet I value each as a steppingstone into higher spirituality. Each gave me clues about where to go next on my spiritual path, but none gave me a definitive direction to go or showed me how to get to my final destination.

And none gave me the feeling of unity with all humankind. Each maintained separateness of some sort. The Goleta and California groups fostered the idea we were better than mainstream churches because we had laid the restrictions of organized church aside. My academic training made us scholars feel superior to the uneducated because we knew the Bible as originally written. My role as a pastor put me above the other members of my church because of my religious training.

Yet my vision remained of a higher spiritual goal, one that let me feel the unity with God and with every other person. I had experienced it once; I knew I could capture it again. And so I continued on my search through my church, questioning long-held assumptions, discarding outdated thinking, embracing new ideas that worked.

We are one, already, in both our flesh history and in our spiritual connection. Inside each of us, we have the Spirit to be exalted. For some, we must discover it; and for all, we must express it in joy and love and forgiveness. The hope is we flow into compassion for all as we move along our journey and ultimately mature into unconditional love throughout the world.

Thank you for walking along this path with me. We have come out of darkness into light, out of fear into love, and out of sorrow into spiritual joy. Let us carry on in Spirit.